The Kentuckians: A Novel

John Fox

THE KENTUCKIANS

A Novel

BY

JOHN FOX, Jr.

AUTHOR OF "A CUMBERLAND VENDETTA"
"HELL FER SARTAIN" ETC.

ILLUSTRATED

BY W. T. SMEDLEY

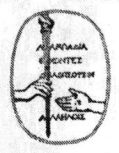

NEW YORK AND LONDON
HARPER & BROTHERS PUBLISHERS
1898

By JOHN FOX, Jr.

"HELL FER SARTAIN," and Other Stories. Post 8vo, Cloth, Ornamental, Uncut Edges, $1 00.
A CUMBERLAND VENDETTA, and Other Stories. Illustrated. Post 8vo, Cloth, Ornamental, $1 25.

NEW YORK AND LONDON:
HARPER & BROTHERS, PUBLISHERS.

Copyright, 1897, by HARPER & BROTHERS.

All rights reserved.

Printing Statement:

Due to the very old age and scarcity of this book, many of the pages may be hard to read due to the blurring of the original text, possible missing pages, missing text, dark backgrounds and other issues beyond our control.

Because this is such an important and rare work, we believe it is best to reproduce this book regardless of its original condition.

Thank you for your understanding.

"'HE'S IN JAIL'"

TO
MY FATHER
AND
MY FATHER'S KENTUCKIANS

ILLUSTRATIONS

"'HE'S IN JAIL'" . . . . *Frontispiece*

"A PROPHET WAS AMONG THEM" . . . *Facing p.* 4

"THE TWO STEPPED FROM THE GREEK
    PORTICO INTO THE SUNLIGHT" . .   "   8

"MARSHALL WENT AT ONCE TO THE
    PIANO" . . . .   " 82

"HE TOSSED HIS WEAPON ASIDE" . . .   " 180

"'I KNOW WHAT YOU THOUGHT'" . . .   " 222

THE KENTUCKIANS

I

THE people of the little Kentucky capital do not often honor the gray walls of their state-house. The legislators play small part in the social life of the town. A member must have blood, as well as gifts unusual, who can draw from the fine old homes a people with a full century of oratory and social distinction behind them, and, further back, the proud traditions of Virginia. For years young Marshall was the first to quite fill the measure, and he was to speak that afternoon. The ladies' gallery was full, and the Governor's daughter, Anne, sat midway. About her was a sudden flutter and a leaning forward when Marshall strode a little consciously down the aisle and took his seat. When he rose to speak, the quick silence of the House was a tribute to thrill him.

It was oratory that one hears rarely now, even in the South. There was an old-fashioned pitch to the vibrant voice, the fire of strong feeling in the fearless eye, an old-fashioned grace and dignity of manner, and a dash that his high color showed to be not wholly natural. The speech was old-fashioned, emotional, the sentences full, swinging, poetic, rich with imagery and classical allusion. And always—in voice, eye, bearing, and gesture —was there gallant consciousness of the gallery behind. More than once his eyes swept the curve of it; and when he came to pay his unfailing tribute to the women of his land, he turned quite around, until his back was upon the Speaker and his uplifted face straight towards the Governor's daughter, who moved her idle fan and colored as many an eye was turned from him to her.

The Speaker's gavel lay untouched before him when the last period rang through the chamber. It would have been useless against the outbreak of applause that followed. Marshall had flamed anew from an already brilliant past. Anne was leaning back with luminous eyes and a proud heart. The gallant old Governor himself was hurrying from under the gallery to bend over his protégé and grasp his hand. The pit of the House buzzed like a hive of bees. Down there a Greek passion for oratory was still alive; in the older men the young fellow stirred memories that were sacred; and the hum rose so high that the sharp rap of the gavel went through it twice unnoticed, then twice again, more sharply still. The Speaker's face was turned to one dark corner of the room where, under the big clock, stood the rough figure of a mountaineer, with hands behind him and swaying awkwardly from side to side, as though his tongue were refusing him utterance. Once he cleared his throat huskily, and a smile started on many a face, and quickly stopped, for it was plain that the man's trouble was not embarrassment, but some storm of feeling that threatened to engulf his brain and surge out in a torrent of invective. The mountaineer himself seemed fearful of some such thing; for, with turbulent calmness, he began slowly, and went on with great care. No reason was apparent, but at the sound of his voice the House turned towards him with the silence of premonition. One by one wrinkles came into the Speaker's strong, placid face. Marshall, quick to feel merit and generous to grant it, had straightened in his chair. The old Governor, going out, was halted by the voice at the door.

"A PROPHET WAS AMONG THEM"

And one, who himself loved the Governor's daughter, remembered long afterwards that she leaned suddenly towards the man, with her eyes wide and her face quite tense with absorption. The secret was in more than his simple bigness, more than his massive head and heavy hair, in more even than the extraordinary voice that came from him. It was an electric recognition of force—the force with which Nature does her heavy work under the earth and in the clouds; and here and there an old member knew that a prophet was among them.

It was the old fight—patrician against plebeian, crude force against culture—but the House knew that young Randolph Marshall, who already challenged the brilliant traditions of a great forefather, who was a promise to redeem a degenerate present and bring back a great past, had found an easy peer in the awkward bulk just risen before them, unknown.

There was little applause when the mountaineer was done. The surprise was too great, the people were too much moved. Adjournment came at once, and everybody asked who the man was, and nobody could tell. One member, who still stood gripping his own wrist hard, recalled on a sudden the recent death of a mountain representative; and, on a sudden, the old Governor at the door remembered that he had signed credentials for somebody to take a dead member's place. This was the man. Outside, Anne Bruce came slowly down the oval stone stairway, and at the bottom Marshall was waiting for her. She smiled a little absently when he raised his hat, and the two stepped from the Greek portico into the sunlight and, passing slowly under the elms and out the sagging iron gate, turned towards the old Mansion. On the curb-stone, just outside, stood one of the figures familiar to the streets of the capital, a man in stripes—a "trusty" on parole—whose square sullen jaw caught Anne's attention sharply, as did the sign of force in a face always. A moment later, the big mountaineer stopped there and talked kindly with the convict awhile. Then, still in a tremor, he moved on alone, across the town and through the old wooden bridge over the river, then out to Devil's Hollow and the hills.

II

The sun must climb mountains first— the Cumberland range, that grim and once effectual protest against the march of the race westward. Over this frowning wall, the first light flashes down through primitive woods and into fastnesses that hold the sources of great rivers and riches unimagined, under and on the earth; beyond, it slants the crests of lesser hills and bushy knolls that sink by-and-by to the gentle undulations of bluegrass pasture and woodland; south and west then, catching the spire of convent and monastery, over fields of pennyroyal, and finally through the Purchase — last clutch of the Spaniard—to light up the yellow river that holds a strange mixt-

"THE TWO STEPPED FROM THE GREEK PORTICO INTO THE SUNLIGHT"

ure of soils and people in the hollow of its arm.

Something more than a century ago the range gave way a little, as earth and water must when the Anglo-Saxon starts, but only to say, "You may pass over and on, but what drops behind is mine; and I hold my own." To-day its woods are primeval, its riches are unrifled, and its people are the people of another age—for the range has held its own.

These men of the mountains and the people of the blue-grass are the extremes of civilization in the State. Through the brush country they can almost touch hands, and yet they know as little and have as little care of one another as though a sea were between them. A few years ago there was but one point where they ever came in contact, one point where their interests could clash. That was the capital, the lazy little capital, on both sides of the river between the big sleepy hills, with its old, gray wooden bridge, its sturdy old homes, its State buildings of gray stone and classic porticos, and its dead asleep, up in the last sunlight, around the first great Kentuckian — the hunter Boone. There the river links highland with lowland like an all but useless artery, barren hill-side with rich pastureland, blue-grass with rhododendron, deterioration with slow progress, darkness with light that sometimes is a little dim, the present century with the last. The big hills about the town are little mountains that have followed the river down from the great highlands, and have brought with them mute messengers — mountain trees, mountain birds, and mountain flowers — to ask that the dark region within be not wholly forgot, and to show that the wish of nature at least is for brotherhood. Down this river come wild raftsmen, who stalk along the middle of the street, single file and curiously subdued;

who climb through the car windows, and are swept through the blue-grass, to trudge the old Wilderness Road back home. Here are two points of close contact for the mountaineer and the lowlander—the legislature and the penitentiary. Thirty miles away is an old university—the first college built west of the Alleghanies—where a mountaineer drifted in occasionally to learn to teach or to preach. Nowhere else and in no way else had the extremes ever touched, until now, for the first time in history, they were in conflict.

A feud—one of those relics of mediæval days that had been held like a fossil in the hills—had broken out afresh. It was called the Keaton-Stallard "war" in the mountains, and it had been giving trouble a long while. Recently the county judge had been driven from the court-house, and the Attorney-General of the State had gone with soldiers to hold court at the county-seat. The only verdict rendered during the term was against the General himself for carrying a weapon concealed; and a heavy fine was imposed for the same, which the Governor had to remit. Meanwhile the feudsmen were out in the brush, waiting. When the soldiers went back to the blue-grass, they came out from their hiding-places and began over again. Now it was worse than ever. The Keatons had got the Stallards besieged not long since, and the Keaton leader tried to get a cannon. In good faith, and with a humor that was mighty because unconscious, he had tried to purchase one from the State authorities— from the Governor himself. Judge, jailer, sheriff, and constable were involved now, and the county was nearing anarchy.

The reputation of the State was at issue, and civilization in the blue-grass was rebuking barbarism in the mountains. Abolish the county, was the cry at the capital, and that afternoon Marshall had voiced it. He had been taken off guard. He had gone down the current of tradition, catching up straws that are anybody's for the catching—stock allusions to wolf-scalps and pauperism; scathing mountain lawlessness as a red blot on the 'scutcheon of the State, which, to quote the spirit of his talk, had stained the highland border of the commonwealth with blood, and abroad was engulfing the reputation of the lowland blue-grass; contrasting, finally, the garden-spot of the earth, his own land of milk and honey, with the black ribs of rock and forest that still harbor the evil spirit of the Middle Ages. It had never been better done, for under the humor and easy good-nature of the speech were a quivering pride of State and a bitter arraignment of the people who were bringing it into disrepute. The mountaineer was a straggler, a deserter from the ranks. He was vicious, untrustworthy, ignorant, lawless, and content with his degradation. He was idle, shiftless, hopeless; a burden to the State, a drawback to civilization. That was the plain truth under Marshall's courteous words, and, well told as it was, it would have been better told had he known the presence of the rough champion who, answering just that truth, tore apart his loose net-work with the ease of summer lightning lifting the horizon at dusk. His was a voice from the wilderness; it bespoke a new and throbbing power in the destiny of the State; it proclaimed a commercial epoch. He admitted much, he denied somewhat, he made little defence, and he apologized not at all. His appeal was for fairness — that was all; and it was fierce, passionate, and tender. He was a mountaineer. He lived in the county under discussion, in the town where the feud was going on. More, an uncle of his had once been a leader of the Stallard faction. His people were idle, shiftless, ignorant, lawless. No wonder. They had started as backwoodsmen a century ago; they had lived apart from the world and without books, schools, or churches since the Revolution; they had had a century of such a life in which to deteriorate. Their law was lax. They lived apart from one another as well, and, of necessity, public sentiment was weak and unity of action difficult—except for mischief. It was easy for ten bad men to give character to a community—to embroil ninety good ones. And that was what had been done. The good ninety were there for every ten that were bad. Nobody deplored the feud more than he, but he saw there were times when people must take the law into their own hands. The mountain people must in the end govern themselves, and they could not begin too soon. To disrupt the county would be to take away the only remedy possible in the end. Then the heavy brows lifted, and a surprising challenge came. By what right and from what high place did the people of the blue-grass rebuke the people of the mountains? Were they less quick to fight? In one section, the fighting was by individuals; in the other, families and friends for a good reason took up the quarrel. Was not that the great difference? And for whom was there the less excuse? For the people who knew, or for the ignorant; for them who could enforce the law, or for them who, because of their environment, were almost helpless? Who knew how powerful that environment had been? Who knew that it did not make the mighty distinctions between the mountaineers and the people of the blue-grass; that the slipping of a linchpin in a wagon on the Wilderness Road had not made the difference between his own family and the proudest in the State; that the gentleman himself was not scoring his own kin? Why not? And with stirring queries like these he closed like a trumpet over the future of his much-mocked hills when their riches were unlocked to their own people and to the outer world. It was the man that made the sensation. What he said, at another time and from another source, would have got scant attention and no credence. But two facts spoke for him now: already a tide of speculation was turning into those little known hills, and there before the House was at least one human product of them who plainly could force the question to be handled with serious care.

It was the power of the speech that stung Marshall. The matter of it was of little moment to him. Once in a while he had chased a red fox from the bluegrass to the foot-hills. As a boy, he had gone with his father on annual trips to the Cumberland to fish and to hunt deer.

The Marshalls even owned mountain lands somewhere, which, with their sole crop of taxes, had been a jest in the family for generations. That was the little he knew of his own mountains. He had cared even less; but, while he listened, his sense of fairness made him quickly sorry that he had spoken with such confidence when there was room for any doubt; and before the mountaineer was done he was silently and uneasily measuring strength with him, point by point.

To Anne, the man and the speech were a revelation: she barely knew her State had mountains. She hardly spoke on her way home, and she seemed not to notice Marshall's unusual silence.

"He has the fascination of something new and perhaps terrible," she said once. "And it's startling, what he said. I wonder if it can be true?" And again, a moment later, slowly: "It is very strange; it all seems to have happened before."

Marshall's answer was a little grim:
"Once is enough for me, I think."

"You and your speech," she went on, barely heeding his interruption. "It seemed as though I had already heard you make just that speech under just those circumstances. It's one of those queer experiences that seem to have occurred before, down to minute details."

"That was the trouble," said Marshall, quietly. "I made that speech, practically, on my graduating-day. I hadn't studied the question since."

Anne's face cleared. "Oh, that's the explanation! A thing seems to have happened before, I suppose, because it has so nearly happened that it seems to be exactly the same thing."

"Yes," assented Marshall, but he was watching Anne steadily. He was already smarting with humiliation, and it hurt him that she could be so absorbed as to carelessly press the thorn in his flesh still farther in, and apparently not guess or not care how it rankled.

"Once even that man's face seemed familiar," she added. "I'd like to know all about him." They had reached the steps of the Mansion, and Marshall was taking off his hat.

"Make him tell you."

Anne looked up quickly. "I will."

"Good-bye."

Anne smiled. She was accustomed to that tone; she had forgiven it many times; she had been distrait, and she would forgive it again. "Good-bye," she said, gently.

III

It was Saturday, and Marshall always spent Sunday at home. It was the run of an hour to Lexington on the fast train, and at sunset he was in a buggy, behind a little blooded mare, and on one of the white turnpikes that make a spider's web of the blue-grass, speeding home. A red arc of the sun was still visible just behind the statue of the great Commoner, and across the long, low sky one cloud in the east was still rosy with light. Already the dew was rising, and when he swept down over a little bridge in a hollow the air was deliciously cool and heavy with the wet fragrance of mint and pennyroyal. On either side the vespers of a song-sparrow would radiate now and then from the top of a low weed, and a meadow-lark would rise and wheel, singing, towards the west. Marshall's chin was almost on his breast. The reins were loose, and the noble little mare was plying her swift legs so easily under her that her high head and shining back gave hardly a sign of effort. She let the dark have barely time to settle over the rolling fields before she stopped of her own accord at her master's home gate. Marshall got out with some difficulty, and, without a word of command, she walked through the gate and waited for him to climb in. The buggy made no noise on the thick turf, and no one was in sight when he reached the stiles.

"Tom!"

"Yessuh!"

The voice came from a whitewashed cabin behind a clump of lilac, and an old negro shuffled hastily after it. The young fellow's voice was impatient. A woman's figure appeared in the doorway under the sunrise window-light as Marshall climbed the stiles.

"Rannie!"

"Yes, mother," he answered; and he held his breath while she kissed him. It was a big hall that he entered, with a graceful, semi-Oriental arch midway, and two doors opening on either side. The parlor was lighted, and through its door old furniture and old portraits were visible; and ancient wall-paper, brought from England a century since, blue in color, with clouds painted under the high ceiling, and an English stag - chase running entirely around the four walls. The ring of girlish laughter came down the stairway as Marshall passed into the dining-room. His mother had gathered in a little house-party of girls from the neighborhood, as she often did, to brighten his home-coming. Supper was over, and they were awaiting the arrival of young men from town. Marshall ate little and had little to say, and very slowly a shadow passed over his mother's brow and eyes.

"What's wrong, my son?" she asked, quietly.

"Nothing, mother, nothing. Don't bother." He laughed slightly. "Maybe it's because I've got a rival."

His mother smiled.

"Oh no, not with her"—he laughed again—"at least, not yet. A man beat me speaking this afternoon. He took me by surprise, but I'll be ready for him next time. Still, I'm not very well, and I can't go into the parlor to-night. Besides, I've got some writing to do. Tell them how sorry I am, won't you?" He rose from his seat, for he could hear the coming guests in the hall. "Good-night," he said; and he kissed her forehead as he passed behind her chair, but the shadow that was there stayed.

A little darky girl in a checked cotton dress lighted his way outside along a path of round-stone flagging. For the house was built after the earliest colonial fashion, with an ell left and right—one of which, disconnected from the house and called the "office" in slavery days, had been Marshall's room since the day he started to town to school. It signified paternal trust; it meant independence. His room was ready. The student-lamp was lighted. On the table was a vase of flowers from his mother's garden, and he sat down close to their fragrance, and, with a conscious purpose of fulfilling his word, he did try for a while to write. But his hand shook, and he arose and opened a pantry door to one side of the fireplace, and called from the window for old Tom to bring him drinking-water. The glisten of glass-ware came through the crack of the pantry door, and the old negro gave it one sullen glance and went out without speaking. Marshall was walking up and down the room. Once he stopped at the mantel to look at the picture of a very young girl in white muslin and with a big Leghorn hat held lightly by one slender hand in her lap. Under it was a scrawling line, "To Rannie from Anne." He turned sharply away and sat down at his table again, with his forehead on his crossed arms. There had been no trouble, no doubt, between the two in those young days. Now there seemed to be nothing else; and it was in one of these wretched intervals of causeless misunderstanding that a hulking countryman had taught him his first bitter lesson in defeat while Anne looked on. They were having a good time in the parlor. Somebody was playing a waltz. There was a ripple of light laughter through the hall door, and some deep-voiced young fellow was talking low on the porch not far from his window. The sounds smote him with a sharp pain of remoteness from it all, and straightway a memory began to bridge the gap between him and those other days; so that he rose presently and took down the picture and put it on the table before him, looking at it steadily. In a little while he unlocked a drawer at his right hand, and took out a note-book and began with the beginning, slowly turning the leaves. It was filled with his own manuscript. Here and there was a verse, "To Anne." On every page, from every paragraph, the name sprang from the white paper — Anne! Anne! Anne! He had meant to burn that book; the impulse came now, as always; but now, as always, he went on turning the leaves. It ran back years — to the childhood of the girl. "Her father's brain, her mother's heart," ran one line, "but her beauty is her own." Some of the verse was almost good. It was Anne's brow here, her eyes there, her mouth, her hand, her arm; "that arm," he read, smiling faintly — "the little hollow midway from which the gracious lovely lines start up and down. It would hold the rain a snowdrop might catch; dew enough for the bath — the ivory bath — of a humming-bird; enough nectar to make Cupid delirious, were he to use it for a drinking-cup. Looking for Psyche, the little god rests there, no doubt, while she sleeps. If he doesn't, he is blind indeed."

Those were the days when he thought he might be a poet or a novelist if either were a manlier trade; if there were not always the more serious business of law and politics to which he was committed by inheritance. Still it was very foolish, the book, and with the impulse again to burn, he placed it back in the drawer and turned the key. Then he put the picture in its place, and sat down again, as though he would go on with his work, but, instead, reached suddenly across the table. The sound of old Tom's banjo was coming up through his back window from the lilacs below, and, as his fingers closed around the glass, the strum started up before him the old array of ever-weakening visions—the negro's reproachful look, the deepening shadows in his mother's face, the pain in Anne's clear eyes—and now a new one, the figure of the mountaineer, burly, vivid, and so menacing that he felt nerve, muscle, and brain get suddenly tense as though to meet some shock. And there was his hand trembling like an old man's under the green shade of the lamp. The sight smote him through with a fear of himself so sharp that he brushed his hands rapidly across his eyes, and with tightened lips once more took up his pen.

The moon looked in at his window radiantly when he pushed the curtains aside to close a shutter, so that he changed his mind about going to bed, and blew out his lamp and sat at the window, looking out. The young men were going home. He heard the laughing good-byes in the hall, and the low, laughing talk of the young fellows where they were unhitching their horses behind the shrubbery; then the soft beat of hoofs and wheels on the turf, the loud slam of the pike gate, and the wild rush of the young bucks racing each other home. There was a rustle in the hall, the closing of a door below, a shutter above, and the house was still.

Not a breath of air moved outside. The white aspens were quiet as the sombre aged pines that had been brought over from old Hanover, in Virginia, and stood with proud solemnity befitting the honor. Across the meadow came the low bellow of a restless bull; nearer, the tinkle of a sheep-bell; and closer, the drowsy twitter of birds in the lilac-bushes at the garden gate. Beyond the lawn and the mock-orange hedge was the woodland, with its sinuous line of soft shadow against the sky, and the broken moonlight under its low branches. Primitive soil, that woodland; no plough had run a furrow through it; no white man had called it his own before the boy's great forefather, asleep under the wrinkled pines. How full of peace it was—how still!

Over in the other ell, his mother had gone to sleep with the last prayer on her lips, the last thought in her heart, for him. She had taken him with her into dreamland, no doubt. She was affected, his mother, so a teasing old aunt had told him—and her; but never in his life could he remember her perfect poise of body and soul to waver, her sweet dignity to unbend. Proud, but very gentle, her face was—he knew but one other like it. "To be your father's wife and your mother, my son," he had heard her, in simple faith, once say. That was her mission on earth. And what a mission he was making for that gracious life!

In the dark parlor, just through the

wall of his room, were Jouett portraits of his kinspeople—of the great Marshall, whose great day people said he was to bring back. Next him was that Marshall's youngest son, a proud-looking young fellow with a noble face and a quiet smile, who had died early, and who, the old aunt said, was the more brilliant of the two. Rannie was like that great-uncle, she used often to say. And he, Marshall knew, had quietly and with beautiful dignity drunk himself to death for a woman. Men could do that in his day. Men had—the young fellow rose, shivering from another reason than the cooling night air; it still was possible.

Over the quiet fields of blue-grass and young wheat and blossoming clover, in the capital, Boone Stallard was looking from his window on the prison, white in the moonlight as a sepulchre, and on the bleak cliff rising behind it; and his last thoughts, too, were on his home and his people: the old two-roomed log cabin with its long porch and long slanting roof, Black Mountain rising in a sheer wall of green behind it, and a little creek tinkling under laurel and rhododendron into the Cumberland; his mother, gaunt, aged, in brown homespun, with her pipe, in a corner of the fireplace; opposite, his sister—whose husband had been killed in the feud—with a worn pallid face and dull eyes; his half-brother, cleaning his Winchester, no doubt; the children in bed; the talk of the feud, always the feud. They were all Stallards on that creek, just as in the next bend of the river all were Keatons—their hereditary enemies. They were "a high-heeled and overbearin' race," the Stallards were; and they were hated and fought, and they hated and fought back, with the end not yet come. All his life, Boone Stallard had known only hardship, work, self-denial. There was no love of sloth, no vice of blood, to stunt his growth; as yet, no love of woman to confuse his purpose, nor inspire it.

Not once did the two currents cross but on the thinkers themselves; on nothing else—not even on Anne.

IV

A week later the Mansion was thrown open, for the third time during the session, to the law-makers and their wives. Stallard, Colton said, must go; and Colton's word, now, was to the good-natured mountaineer little short of law.

He had found an unknown ally when he opened the great Kentucky daily on the morning after his first fight. There was a long account of the debate, a strong tribute to "The Cumberland Cyclone," as Colton, the correspondent, called him, and an editorial on the question that bore the distinctive ear-marks of the great man in charge. That same morning, when the question of disruption came up, a member who had considerable aspiration, some foresight, and no principles to make or mar his future, and who knew he would help himself in another section and not harm himself in his own, rose and took sides with Stallard, emphasizing the editor's emphasis of Stallard's idea that the mountain people must some day govern themselves, and, therefore, would be better let alone now. To the surprise of all, Marshall rose and stated frankly the lack of positive knowledge on which he had spoken the day before. While he must hold to certain opinions expressed, he recognized the possibility of having done the mountain people wrong in certain statements made; that time would soon prove.

Meanwhile, he would withdraw his motion, with the consent of the House, and counsel further forbearance on the part of the State. It was graceful, magnanimous, gallant; but Colton, watching the mountaineer's face, saw not a muscle of it move. Marshall's bill was put aside for the time. The mountain members, headed by Jack Mockaby, drew close to Stallard and, before noon of his second day at the capital, Stallard found himself a man of mark, and with a following that in all legislative questions could exact consideration. And for the hour of that noon his head swam and got steady again; for his brain was as sane as his purpose was firm. Of his gift of oratory, he took as little thought as a bird takes of its gift of song. He neither drank nor gambled, and as he kept aloof from all social affairs, he wasted neither his energy nor his time. Few committees of importance were appointed upon which he did not have a place, and his capacity for work was prodigious. In Colton he came at once to know his best friend, and every few days he saw his name prominent in the reports of legislative doings. These would slowly make their way home to the mountains, and Stallard knew his seat was secure for another term unless the feud intervened. Once even, in the first flush of his success, the dome of the big Capitol floated a little while along the horizon of his heated vision, and sank. For Stallard's second thought and his last were ever for his people; and he watched their welfare with an eye that let no measure escape that might be of possible help to them. Thus far he had given no thought to anything but work, and now Colton said that, out of respect to the Governor who had been kind to him, Stallard must go to the Mansion. So he had dressed himself in his best—which was quite bad —had walked twice past the brilliantly lighted old house, and in hopeless indecision had started, for the second time, home. Inside, Anne sat in a corner of the big square drawing-room, watching the late-coming guests. Colton was on the sofa beside her and Marshall stood just to one side. The two men did not like each other, and for that reason Colton rattled on in his talk recklessly. The receiving-line of young women in white was broken, and the rather chill formality of the occasion dissolved. Occasionally some little woman, tripping past, would ask, naïvely, "Oh, you haven't met my husband?" And off she would go for the embryonic statesman. Dress and manners made Anne shudder now and then, but no sign arose above the fine courtesy that made social democracy in her own home absolute; and, unfailingly, she presented Marshall, who bowed with perfect gravity to the absurd little ducks and curtseys made him. Colton, who knew everybody, was giving pen-and-ink sketches right and left.

They were all there—from the Peavine to the Purchase, through blue-grass, bear-grass, and pennyroyal; from Mammoth Cave and Gethsemane, the Knobs and the Benson Hills; from aristocratic Fayette and Bourbon, "sweet Owen" fortress of democracy, to border Harlan, hot-bed of the feud; from the Mississippi to Hell-fer-Sartain Creek in bloody Breathitt. Those were the contrasting soils, social sections, and divisions of vegetation on which the devil was said to have slyly put a thumb of reservation when he offered the earth to his great Conqueror ("and sometimes," said Colton, "I think the reservation was granted"). All this the magic name of old Kentucky meant to her loyal sons, who are to this country what the Irishman is to the world; and who, no matter where cast, remain what they were born—Kentuckians—to the end. The Virginia cavalier was there, he went on, with a side-glance at Marshall; the Scotch-Irishman, who had taken on the cavalier's polish and lost nothing of his own strength; the "pore white trash"—now risen in the world; the kinless nondescript—himself, for instance; the political grandee of the cross-roads—he of the Clay manner and the Websterian brow across the room. He always made afternoon calls in his dress suit. There was Jack Mockaby from Breathitt, who was expecting arrest each day last year, for a little feud of his own, while he was in the House making laws for the rest of the State. The gaunt individual at the door was another mountaineer. He had brought his wife with him to the "settlemints." Once she had been asked if she were going to the theatre. She "'lowed she was, but she didn't aim to take part." And she did go, and she took down her hair before the curtain went up, gave it a little brush or two, and slowly rolled it up in a knot at the back of her head. On a fishing trip, Colton had taken dinner with one of this member's constituents. They had corn-bread and potatoes.

"Take out, stranger," said the mountaineer. "Hev a tater; take two of 'em; take damn nigh all of 'em."

Oh, they were a strange people, these mountaineers — proud, hospitable, good-hearted, and murderous! Religious, too: they talked chiefly of homicide and the Bible. He knew of an awful fight that came up over a discussion on original sin. Yes, they were queer; but there was one— Boone Stallard was his name—Miss Anne had heard him speak? Colton thought he could make something of him.

"They call him the 'Cumberland Cyclone' now: that's mine, that phrase. Pretty good, isn't it? They will run him against Marshall for Speaker next year," he added, with innocent malice; "mark my words. He's a coming man—but he doesn't seem to be coming here very fast. He said he would. If he doesn't show up in five minutes, I'm going after him. It'll be his début, and I'm his chaperon. Ah—"

The information was not worth while. Though smilingly interested in Colton's light nonsense, she was glancing now and then at the door, where her father was receiving the last stragglers; and, looking at her, Marshall knew when she saw the mountaineer, and he smiled: her interest amused him. Stallard's big form was in the doorway. His eyes were roving helplessly up and down the room, and his face, despite its gravity, wore so pained a look that the girl herself half rose. But the Governor had stepped forward and, holding the new-comer's arm, was leading him across the room towards her.

"Anne, I want to present Mr. Stallard to you—Mr. Boone Stallard. Mr. Marshall, Mr. Stallard—you two should know each other; and Mr. Colton you know, of course."

The girl put out her hand. Marshall, with punctilious courtesy, was putting out his when he met Stallard's eye. The mountaineer knew no polite law that bade him, feeling one way, to act another; and what he felt, he made plain. Marshall straightened like steel. It was a declaration of war, open, mutual; and Colton, with a quick breath, half rose from his seat. The Governor, turning away, saw nothing, and Anne's eyes were lowered suddenly to the white point of one of her slippers.

"Pardon," said Marshall, with quick tact; "your father is calling me." And he bowed himself away and towards the Governor, who was passing through the door.

Colton turned to Anne's friend, Katherine Craig, who sat at his right, and whose eyes had lost nothing. Stallard crossed his big hands awkwardly in front of him, and stood with one foot advanced and the knee bent. He wore a great Prince Albert coat, which was longer in front than behind, and high boots which showed to their tops under his trousers. They were carefully blackened, and the feet were large—so was the man. Anne saw all these details before she raised her eyes to his, and then for a while she quite forgot them. They were calm, open eyes that she saw, quite dark but luminous, and they quietly held hers in a way that made her wonder then whether it might not be hard for some woman, against his will, to turn her own aside. Yet they were timid too, and kindly, while the strong mouth was for the moment hard; it still held the antagonism that elsewhere in the rugged face was gone.

"I heard your speech," she said, friendlily. "I want to congratulate you. You gave us all a surprise—especially Mr. Marshall."

"Well, I am very glad you liked it," he said, slowly and with great care, almost as if he were speaking another tongue. "I don't recollect that I saw you there. I reckon I didn't look around at the gallery."

"No," she said, with a smile; "you were not very gallant."

She was sorry when the words left her mouth, the big man looked so helpless. But no woman minds if the strong are shy, and she went on a little blindly: "Now Mr. Marshall paid us a pretty compliment." If she were uncertain as to the little start he gave when she mentioned Marshall's name just before, she was not now. The repression at his lips spread to his eyes, his brow, and his nostrils, and he did not look pleasant. She did not know why she should press the point further, but the impulse was irresistible.

"Mr. Marshall is a great friend of mine," she added, her self-control fluttering, and she raised her eyes to see what should come into his, and she was frightened. She knew little of the strict ethics that governed his life in the matter of friendship; if Marshall was her friend, then she was the mountaineer's enemy; but with a flash she caught the thought in his mind and, with it, too, his suspicion that she had meant to make the fact of her friendship for Marshall plain.

"I hope you two will like each other," she added, quickly, and with a vague purpose of somehow putting herself to rights; but the mountaineer stared merely.

"I don't think we will," he said, bluntly. Again Anne's eyes went for refuge back to the point of her slipper, and luckily for both, just then, the Governor came to take Stallard away. Colton and Katherine turned.

"How did you get along?" asked Colton. Anne laughed. Her cheeks were a bright red, and Colton began to wonder.

"Not very well. It was dreadful. He's half a savage. He made me afraid."

Marshall was coming up behind her, and could not help but hear what pleases no lover — fear in a woman of another man. His manner was light and spirited, and he laughed in a way that made her look sharply up.

"Good-night." His face was flushed, and Anne's hardened a little while she looked after him. Stallard did not come to bid her good-night, and she guessed the truth—that he did not know it was necessary. Still he should have wanted to come, she thought, imperiously; and she did not guess the truth of that—that, much puzzled, he had wanted to come; that he had passed the rear door to look at her, and had stood a long while, staring at her strangely; that he had hesitated, through sheer fear, to speak to her again, and, vaguely distressed, had slipped away without a word to anybody.

For a long while, after the guests were gone, she sat thinking under the pink drop-light in her father's study. It had been the same thing over and over for so long with Marshall—peace, a foolish quarrel, the wine-room and the card-table; some wild deed, contrition, pardon, and peace again. It was the beginning of the second stage now, and she looked a little bitter, and then she sighed helplessly, as though she would as well make ready now to forgive him again. When she thought of Stallard, she found herself going back again to Marshall's graduating-day. That was odd, but the fact slipped unnoticed through her consciousness, for she was wishing that Marshall had the strength that she believed was the mountaineer's. What might he not do then? Then, perhaps, everything might be otherwise. And thinking of the mountaineer again, there came again, out of the past, the hot air of the old university hall; and now, as then, she was walking out on the big portico to escape it. That day she had dropped her parasol down the great flight of stone steps. A rough-looking country boy was leaning against one of the big pillars, staring at her. She waited for him to pick it up, but he never took his eyes from her face, and she got it herself.

She had thought him stupid and impolite, and she never knew what fixed the incident in her mind, unless it was the boy's intent stare and his shock of black hair. Even now her memory of the incident had no significance, for she was busy thinking how absurd the contrast was between the mountaineer's face and his dress, and wondering why it was that, once, some look in the man's eyes should have given her such a pang of pity for him. He must have miserably misunderstood her that night, and no wonder; she must make that right, and quickly.

"Papa," she said, "is there any reason why I shouldn't ask that Mr.—Boone—Stallard"—she pronounced the name slowly—"to dinner?"

"Why, no, Anne; why not?"

"Oh, nothing, I didn't know. He's so queer. He's so diffident—it's absurd in such a big man—and then he isn't. I wonder that he came to-night."

"It was Colton's doing, I imagine," said the Governor, rising to fill his pipe; "and then I suppose he thought he owed especial courtesy to me. I let out a pretty bad convict on parole not long ago, at his request—a mountaineer."

"Who is he?" she asked, so absent-mindedly that the Governor turned.

"Who is who?" he answered, smiling; and then, "Why, you remember, surely. Marshall introduced a bill to abolish his county the other day. He belongs to one of the factions that are making trouble in the mountains. I suppose one-fourth of the people in his county have the name of Stallard. And they are worse about stretching kinship down there than we are."

The girl rose to go to her room, and the Governor called to her again, and she stopped under the light of the stairway, with her dreaming face uplifted, the hem of her gown raised from one arched foot, and one white hand on the banister—and nobody there to see!

"By-the-way, can't you make use of a trusty for a day or two in the garden? I'll send you a feudsman, if you are getting interested in the mountaineers. I made still another trusty not long ago, at the warden's request. The mountaineers can't stand confinement, he says, having lived all their lives in the open air. Can you give one something to do?"

Anne's lips parted and her eyes closed sleepily. "Yes," she said.

V

A fortnight later, Anne sat in the shade of her grape-arbor, directing the leisurely labor of the "trusty" who had come over from the gloomy prison whose high gray walls and peaked roof, with its ceaseless column of black smoke, were visible over the houses that sat between.

Her dinner had taken place a few nights before. Stallard was not only not there —he had not even answered her note of invitation. Colton laughed when she told him. He could not explain it, but he knew why the mountaineer had probably not come. Stallard had been hard at work; he was not merely an orator; he shirked no work, and he read law steadily. He had not answered, perhaps, because he did not know the social need of an answer. He might have turned up at the dinner without having sent his acceptance; that was as likely as what he had done. It was all doubtless true, and the girl wanted to believe that it was. Still, it was the harder to believe for the reason that it was altogether of a piece with the usual way of a man who seemed to swerve aside for nothing, and who bore himself towards her as she had all her life borne herself towards all men. And young as she was, Anne's reign had been a long one. Even as a school-girl she had her little local court of sweethearts, which widened rapidly, as she grew older, through the county, through several counties, through even the confines of the State. It was a social condition already passing away; the pretty young queen and the manly young fellows doing her honor with such loyalty—openly, frankly her slaves—to themselves, to one another, and to the world; declaring love one after another in turn, leaving her with a passionate resolution to throw off the yoke, and bending meekly to it again. For usually she kept the lover the friend even after as lover he was hopeless, if the lover ever is. Occasionally, however, some young fellow, a little fiercer than usual, would stalk away through the hall, bang the door a little more loudly, and really come back no more. Then Anne would go to her room and cry half the night through, to learn soon that he had gone elsewhere for solace, and that her place was filled. Soon she could smile when some young heart went broken from her to mend no more; and, thereafter, she cried sometimes only because she was losing a friend. By-and-by some of her courtiers married, some went other ways, but of the original court a few were still left, and of them Marshall was one. He was the oldest, the most faithful and untiring. His strength, aside from birth, was in oratory and politics, for which the girl, coming from a race of lawyers and statesmen, had an innate predilection; so that, in spite of his wild ways, general expectation, which looks to the untiring to win in love, as in everything else, rested on Marshall. Still he had not won, and Anne kept on her placid, queenly way, holding every man her friend because she was fair with all and loved no one less than his rival. What the trouble was, nobody knew precisely—not Marshall—not even Anne. Once her mother, remembering the boy's inheritance, had given her gentle warning against intrusting herself to him; and his reckless way of life kept the warning always in mind. Always, perhaps, Marshall's perfect loyalty had kept her from knowing how strong her own feeling was for him. And then, as she grew older, she slowly came to exact, what few women do, that a man shall be making an honest effort to realize the best that is in him. That Marshall, brilliant and winning as he was, had never done. It was the contrast in this one particular that was helping arouse her interest in the mountaineer. One look in his face, and doubt on that question, as to Stallard, was at rest. Moreover, she had a swift, sympathetic insight into what was best in the humanity around her, and this told her that in this rugged rustic was more hidden power than she had ever found in any one man. He was the first man with whom it had been necessary for her to be the first to hold out her hand, in simple kindliness at the start, and then for the mere self-acknowledged reason that he was the first to reach her intellect, as somebody might some day reach her heart. Necessarily, it was the first time she had met with no response. To say that she was piqued would be absurd; to say that her interest was not deepened would be to say that she was not a woman and not human. She had thought of the man a good deal; she would tell anybody that. She wanted to know of him, and Colton had told her much, and everything was of interest. She knew nothing of the mountains, nothing of the people who lived in them. Since she had lived at the capital, she had watched the raftsmen coming down the river; once, she had seen a crowd of dusty, wild-looking men empty from the train under charge of an officer, and she had been told that they were moonshiners; that was all. No more did she know of the highlands of the east, and no more of the people who sprang from them. But Colton—the subject was getting to be a hobby with him—had told her all he knew and much more. Her personal interest in Stallard helped her interest in his people. He was the first mountaineer she had seen close at hand. The second was in her garden before her, and she had no way of knowing that both were exceptional. The convict was young and rather good-looking. He had a mat of close-cut black hair and a swarthy face. His eyes were dark, bright, open, and frankly curious. The face was almost good, except for the small, loose, beautiful mouth, which, with all its easy good-humor, showed to a close study as sensual and rather cruel. She had hesitated at first about giving him orders.

"Ah, what is your name, please?"

"Buck," he said, without looking at her.

"Buck what?"

"Buck's enough, hain't it?" he said, a little surlily.

"Yes," she said, quietly. "I want you to go on that side and hoe around those rose-bushes there."

The young fellow went to work without a word. The trusties earn their liberty at a sacrifice of the good opinion of their fellow-prisoners; but the young mountaineer was sick for the open air; moreover, he was doing a woman's work under a woman's supervision; and he was not pleased. He worked very well, but he seemed weak. His cheeks soon took on a high color; he breathed hard, and he looked feverish. The stripes must be hot and suffocating, Anne thought on a sudden, and she spoke to him again very kindly.

"You must stop awhile now; the sun is too hot. Sit down there and rest."

The convict sat down readily enough. Anne turned away to look across the street and nod to a passing friend, and, when she turned back, he was looking with boyish directness straight at her.

"Hit's Buck Stallard."

The girl started. Then it dawned that the abrupt giving of his name was an apology, and she smiled.

"You come from Roland County?"

The boy nodded. "Yes," he said.

"That's where all the trouble is going on?"

"Yes." She wondered why he didn't say, "Yes, ma'am." "That's what I'm doin' over thar," he went on, with a jerk of his thumb towards the prison. "Thar's two of us in thar, an' I reckon thar'll be more, ef the boys at home don't watch out."

Most of the prisoners would say they were in for fighting, for manslaughter even, rather than confess to theft or some other petty crime—a curious commentary on the public sentiment within and without the sombre walls. Anne knew that, but she had little doubt that in this case the convict was telling the truth, and she was inured to the point where she did not shrink.

"Ever heerd o' Boone Stallard?"

The question took her off guard, and the next moment she felt herself coloring under the boy's keen look.

"Yes," she said, calmly; "I heard him make a speech the other day."

"Did ye?" he asked, smiling. "Thar hain't nobody as can down Boone on languige. Me an' Boone's kin," he said, a little proudly, but he was watching her closely and feeling his way with care. "We's all kin down thar."

That was what her father had said, and she herself knew what it was to have many kinspeople, and a few of whom she was not proud.

"Has he ever taken part in the feud?" she asked; and again the boy eyed her cautiously.

"Naw," he said, frankly, satisfied with his inspection. "Boone's al'ays a-tryin' to git us fellers to quit. Boone's fer law an' order ever' time, Boone is. Thar hain't nobody down thar like Boone. He ain't afeerd nother. Ever'body knows that. He's plum' crazy 'bout the sanctaty of the law an' his dooty—that's somep'n he picked up from you furriners when he was out in the settlemints, I reckon. He'll git into it some o' these days now, you see; fer he'll go ef he thinks he ought to. An' then thar'll be Billy-hell to pay. You see!"

Again the girl started, but the boy was looking away in complete innocence of giving offence, absorbed no doubt in picturing just what would happen should Boone Stallard some day take part. She remembered, too, that Colton said the mountaineers still talked even before their women with Anglo-Saxon freedom, and that their oaths were little more to them than slang was to the outside world.

"Boone's about the only Stallard as hain't in it; and Stallards air as thick down thar as red-heads in a deadenin'."

"As *what!*"

"Red-heads... woodpeckers—in a deadenin'—a place whar folks have cut the bark off o' trees to kill 'em. The red-heads goes thar 'cause hit's easier fer 'em to peck holes in dead trees. Sometimes I think you furriners knows most ever'thing, an' agin you don't seem to know much." Anne came near laughing aloud. Here was a character.

"What makes you fight that way?"

The boy laughed. "Well, suppose some sorry feller was to shoot your brother or your daddy, an' the high-sheriff was afeerd o' him an' wouldn't arrest him, whut would you do? You know mighty well. You'd just go git yo' gun an' let him have it. That's what. Then mebbe his brother would layway you; an' all yo' folks 'ud git mad an' take hit up; an' things 'ud git frolicsome ginerally. Whut's yo' name?"

The girl had to answer, the question was asked with such frank trust. "Anne Bruce."

The boy repeated the name mechanically, and then looked at the work he had done. "Whut you want to raise so many flowers fer, Anne? Whyn't you put that ground in corn?"

The girl reddened in spite of her amusement. "You must call me Miss Anne or Miss Bruce," she said, quietly.

"Miz Anne," repeated the boy. "Who ever heerd o' sech a thing?" He would have laughed had not her face been so serious. "All right," he said, placidly. "But we don't call no woman 'Miz' whar I come from 'ceptin' they's purty ole or is married. You ain't ole enough, *I* know; an' you ain't married, is ye?"

Anne flushed slightly, but there was not a trace of impudence in his tone, and she could not bring herself to rebuke his childlike curiosity. "No, I'm not married," she said, simply.

But the boy saw something was wrong, and with a look of sudden ill-humor rose to his work. His depression was momentary; he seemed to have the light-hearted irresponsibility of the insane. Already he was humming to himself in a mournful minor; it was something about "wild roses"; the intervals were strange to her ear, and the tune seemed to move through at least three keys. Anne remembered the folk songs that Colton said the mountaineers still sang:

"To jump in the river and drown"—

that was the last sorrowful line; and then he veered to something lively, singing words that she could barely hear:

"Chickens a-crowin' on Sourwood Mountain,
Heh-o-dee-um-dee-eedle-dahdy-dee!
Git yo' dogs an' we'll go huntin',
Heh-o-dee-um-dee-eedle-dahdy-dee!"

It had the darky's rhythm and the darky's way of dropping into the minor on the third line, while the swing of the last was like the far-away winding of a horn, and it was to ring in her ears for years to come. He was changing now, and she smiled. Colton had sung that to her; he called it "The Dying Injunction of Johnnie Buck."

> "Oh, Johnnie Buck is dead,
> An' the last words he said
> Was, never let yo' woman have her way."

There was but one verse, and he sang it over and over while she watched him, trying to realize, to understand, what Colton said; that in this age, this day, this hour; in her own land, her own State, and within the two days' gallop of a thoroughbred of her own home, were people living like the pioneers, singing folk-songs centuries old, talking the speech of Chaucer, and loving, hating, fighting, and dying like the clans of Scotland. It was very strange and interesting, and for no reason she sighed deeply. The town clock was striking noon.

"You'd better go to dinner now," she said, "and come back this afternoon."

"This whut?" The mountaineer's day has no afternoon.

"This evening."

"Aw!" Again the boy laughed frankly. Just then the Governor was passing into the Mansion. "Who is that ole feller?"

"You mustn't say 'old fellow.' You must say 'old gentleman.' That's my father."

"Well, I be durned! Can he pardin me out?"

"Yes, he could, if there were a good reason."

The convict was looking intently at the Governor as he passed through the door. His face had grown sullen and there was a new fire in his eyes.

"An' I never knowed it till yestiddy," he muttered; "an' my time 'most done. Hit ain't right," he said, fiercely.

For the moment he forgot the girl, and he wheeled quickly to her with a sudden fear that he had uncovered himself to a possible enemy, and bent his sharp black eyes full on her. She was puzzled by the change in his face, but she gave him a kindly nod and turned towards the house.

Boone Stallard was passing the gate, as he always did at that hour, going to his dinner. The young trusty called him by his first name and Stallard stopped, but the two did not shake hands. The mountaineer spoke to Anne without raising his hat.

VI

For the time, peace down in the mountains took away the cause of war between Marshall and Stallard at the capital, but hardly a question came up in the House but the tendency was plain in both men to take opposing sides; and always the personal note of enmity was frankly dominant. In consequence, Anne looked forward with some anxiety to the night of her dinner—the dinner to which Stallard had promised to come. He was deeply mortified, Colton told her, over his failure to answer her note; so to show that she forgave him, she had asked him again. She feared nothing openly disagreeable; Marshall would not suffer himself, under her roof, to be drawn into that: still, the mountaineer's blunt hostility might keep her continually on guard and put the table under unpleasant restraint; for the feeling between the two men was public talk, as her interest in the mountaineer was getting to be.

To Marshall, then, she gave the seat of honor. Colton sat on her left. Stallard she placed at her father's right, and next Katherine Craig. A rather talkative newspaper man, a meteor from the North whom Colton had caught while he was still blazing, and who, for Colton's sake, was there, sat midway. Anne could not reckon as to him, being an unknown quantity, and she little dreamed that he was to be the dangerous link of communication which she found necessary to sever with a tactful stroke. He was making a trip through the South to get a comprehensive grasp of the negro question; and, incidentally, to turn a search-light on the origin and condition of the poor whites. That was, in effect, what she heard him tell the Episcopal minister as they were rising to go out to dinner. Now the clergyman, who sat opposite him, was resuming the subject.

"How long shall you stay?" he asked.

"Oh, about six weeks, I suppose," was the careless answer.

"Stay as long as I have," said the minister, with a pleasant smile, "and perhaps you won't write anything."

The journalist realized that he was talking to a Northern man, and his face lighted up.

"Why, how long have you been South?"

"Six years," was the dry answer, and Anne smiled.

Throughout the meal she watched the mountaineer closely. His face was placid and grave, but his eyes were busy. Nothing escaped them. He did nothing that he did not see done first; and she saw him waiting more than once to learn what it was proper to do. It was plain that he would get along; indeed, he had got along. That she noticed when he entered the drawing-room; and now Colton, with the kindliest humor, was calling her attention to the fact, while Marshall was engaged with his right-hand neighbor.

"I've been tempering the cyclone to the shorn lamb of conventionality," he said. "I've got him down out of the clouds now, and he roars gently. I've got his hair cut; and did you observe his patent-leathers? I tied that four-in-hand. He had a ready-made bow of yellow satin. I'll get him out of that Prince Albert pretty soon."

"He surely has improved. How did you manage it so quickly?"

The question was mechanical. She knew Colton as one of the few who can give advice without offence to anybody; but she was watching the Northern journalist, who was vigorously haranguing Reynolds of the geological corps. Several times she saw his lips frame the word "mountaineer."

"Oh, he was easy work. He went to the university at Lexington. But he's been down in the mountains so long since then that he has lapsed into original sin. That's easy, Reynolds says, down there."

Marshall turned just then, and Colton took up the pink maiden on his left. Stallard was not talking much. Most of the time he was shyly listening to Katherine, who was doing her best to engage him, or to the Governor; but now and then he would turn his eyes towards Anne, and she was pleased. Once she gave him a friendly smile and, from his sudden color, she knew that his looking had been unconscious, and that, too, pleased her. The talking was so spirited all round the table that there seemed to be no possible occasion for the two men to come into contact. She began to wonder how she could have feared it: it was hardly possible at the table, and only by accident could they clash in the drawing-room; and then she was quite sure that Colton had warned the mountaineer on this point as well. It was just while she was giving a long sigh of relief that one of those curious lulls came that are said to silence a table of people either twenty minutes before or twenty minutes after the clock strikes an hour. Anne gave a low nervous laugh that made Colton turn quickly towards her. The meteor was sputtering through the sudden quiet.

"No," he said, with emphasis. "The accepted theory of the origin of the mountaineer, particularly of the Kentucky mountaineer, is that he is the descendant—" He had got that far when he became conscious of the intense silence, that everybody was listening, and that Stallard's calm eyes were on him. Anne was trembling when, to her relief, the mountaineer smiled. He had learned a great deal. "— of exported paupers and convicts, indents, and 'pore white trash,'" he said, quietly and quite impersonally. "I don't wonder that the theory has got abroad, because so little is known of the mountaineer and the effect of his environment, but I think—"

"Allow me," said Reynolds, opposite, who was sunbrowned and wore spectacles. "That is a very foolish theory. Some of them are the descendants of those people, of course. There are more of them in the mountains than in the blue-grass, naturally; but the chief differences between them and us come from the fact that they have been shut off from the world absolutely for more than a hundred years. Take out the cavalier element, and, in rank and file, we were originally the same people. Until a man has lived a year at a time in the mountains he doesn't know what a thin veneer civilization is. It goes on and off like a glove, especially off. Put twenty *average* blue-grass families down in the mountains half a dozen miles from one another, take away their books, keep them there, with no schools and no churches, for a hundred years, and they will be as ignorant and lawless as the mountaineer"—with a nod of "saving your presence" to Stallard—"and, with similar causes, fighting one another just the same."

It was a bold speech, but nobody there had the better right to make it, for none there was of better blood. The pure gratitude in Stallard's face was pathetic. Marshall had grown grave, and Anne saw a paleness about his lips.

"You mustn't say a word," she said, seriously, but she spoke too late.

"Would we be assassinating each other from ambush, too?" he asked, with his lids lowered and quietly, but in a way that made Stallard lay down his fork, drop his hands into his lap, and wait.

A look from Anne stopped Reynolds's

answer. "You mustn't go any further now," she said, laughingly, "or I'll have to take part; and I don't know whose part I should take. My great-great-*great*-grandmother lived in a log cabin—didn't she, papa?—and did her own cooking. They went back into the mountains for a while, when game got scarce in the blue-grass. Suppose they had stayed. I might be a mountaineer myself, and be in a feud. Dear me, somebody might be calling me 'pore white trash!'"

The light manner of the girl was serious enough to comfort Stallard unspeakably. It held Marshall back with a humor that had no sting for him. Reynolds was smiling; Colton, dissolved in quiet wonder.

The meteor, after flickering once or twice like a dying tallow dip, had encountered a dangerous light in Stallard's eye and had quite gone out. The storm-cloud was gone, and the men were left to their cigars. Stallard did not smoke, and the

Governor took him to the library, across the hall. Two State senators had Marshall between them over an axe they wanted the lower house to grind. The journalist and the clergyman had drawn together, and Reynolds had Colton and two others at the end of the table, and was telling a story. Anne sat near the folding-doors, which were slightly ajar, and, as the ladies opposite were on some domestic theme and taking in her presence only now and then with a glance, she could not help hearing; and after the first words she frankly listened.

"Maybe you can use it, Colton," Reynolds was saying. "You remember I was captain of the football club at the university? Well, one day, at the beginning of the season, one of the fellows got hurt, and I had to take a green substitute. There were only some Bible students out there looking on—the fellows, you know, who dye their linen dusters for overcoats

in winter—and one of them stepped out.
'I don't know the game, pardner,' he said,
'but I reckon I can tote that ball wherever you wants me.' It was funny to hear
him drawl it out; but he was a big chap,
and I took him. The ball did come to
him presently, and he got it off the ground.
'Whar'd ye say take it?' he asked, holding
it above his head, while two little fellows
on the other side were jumping up after
it like dogs for a piece of bread. 'Run
for the goal!' I yelled. 'Whut, them
stakes?' he drawled. 'Yes, you fool,
run?' He gave me one look as much as
to say, 'Well, I'll attend to you presently'; and then he started, with the ball
in one hand and knocking men right and
left with the other, just as though they
were tenpins, and everybody yelling,
'foul.' He never stopped. One man was
on his back and two were swinging to his
waist, when he was within ten feet of the
goal. He thought he had to go *under* it,

and he staggered those ten feet sidewise and, with the crowd on him, got through. 'Is that the game, pardner?' he asked, when the boys let him up. 'Well, I reckon I can do that all day. Hit's purty hard on a feller's clothes, though.' And we could never get him to play again. He said he hadn't the time, but I believe it was his clothes (we didn't have football suits in those days). He came around to see me about calling him a fool, and I wasn't long apologizing, either. Well, that fellow came over into the College of Arts and turned out a remarkable orator. He actually made his speech at Commencement from a slip of notes in his hand."

Colton was nodding his head. "I remember," he said.

"Well, Colton, that fellow was your cyclone. That was why I stood up for him."

Anne heard Colton's exclamation of surprise, and then no more; but she had been busy with memories, too, and a mystery was clearing. Once more it was Marshall's Commencement day. Again she felt the stifling heat and saw the portico, her parasol on the flight of steps, and the boy against one of the big pillars, with his fixed stare and his head of unruly black hair. The incident came vividly back while Reynolds was telling the story, and she looked at Stallard closely when the men came back into the drawing-room. It was quite possible; she would learn if he were the same. It was an odd cast of fate if he were.

Marshall went at once to the piano to select a song for her. He could both sing and play, but he would rarely do either. Music and art, for men, at least, are yet in serious disfavor through the South, and it is not wise for a man, with the serious purpose of law or politics before him, to show facility in light accomplishments. When Anne sang, Stallard's eyes never left her face. He was leaning against a

"MARSHALL WENT AT ONCE TO THE PIANO"

column at the entrance to the dining-room, with his hands behind him, his shoulders fallen forward, his head sunk back, his lips slightly apart—and once more Anne saw the young rustic against the pillar, and met his curious look again. Only, when she smiled now, there was in his eyes something new, personal, eager, softened, and, on a sudden, a surprised flash of such unreckoning intensity that she faltered in her song, and did not look towards him again. The guests rose to go soon after she was done, but Stallard stood where he was; and when Colton called him by name and he turned, his eyes looked as though he had been suddenly awakened from sleep. The two passed Marshall on their way to Anne, but Stallard seemed not even to see him. He was still looking at Anne, who gave him a friendly, half-frightened smile, and passed him on with Colton. Marshall stayed behind. The mountaineer could hardly find his hat in the hallway and, as he started out, he turned again as though he would go back into the parlor. He seemed dazed.

"I believe—" he said, hesitatingly, and Colton, wondering what the matter was and fearing that he might do some breach of propriety, took him by the arm and led him out the door and into the starlight.

VII

The next week Stallard disappeared altogether. Marshall, too, was rarely in evidence, through a fixed principle of his. One of Anne's suitors had come in from another part of the State, and Marshall, after showing the stranger every possible courtesy, as was his custom with his rivals, hospitably left the field. After the following Sunday, the stranger was gone the way of so many strangers before him, and Marshall smiled and resumed his visits to the Mansion. But Stallard stayed on in hiding. He came once to pay his dinner call, but that was plainly Colton's doing; several others were there, and Anne said nothing to the mountaineer alone. She had asked him to come again, and he had not come. Colton said he was hard at work, Katherine thought him shy, and Anne regretted that she had not been more friendly.

Several times the young trusty had been over to hoe in the garden. Anne made many efforts to find his conscience, to implant therein a seed of regeneration, but she soon gave him up as hopeless. She was astonished by his knowledge of the Scriptures—for sometimes the mountaineer knows the great book from cover to cover—and by the distant application of them to his personal life. He had "heerd all that afore," he said, with some superiority. "He had wrastled with the Sperit, an' he *couldn't* 'come through.' He was jus' a-snortin' fer conviction, he was." Once she asked him why they did not settle their quarrels down in the mountains with their fists instead of with knives and pistols—as though her own people did that.

"All right," he said. "S'posin' a feller does somep'n to you. You go fer him fist an' skull, gougin' an' bitin'. You gits whooped!" he concluded, triumphantly.

"Well," she said, "that isn't a disgrace."

"All right. Then s'posin', the next time he sees ye, he crows over ye. What you goin' to do *then?*"

The problem, aside from religion, which had to be laid aside, was insoluble. The boy was an interesting puzzle to her. He was so frank a heathen. His wickedness was such a thing of impulse and odd reasoning. His curiosity was so absurdly childlike, so removed from impertinence. He never made a word of thanks for the little things she gave him, and yet she saw that he was not unappreciative. He repressed his frankness of speech a good deal, and he showed his consideration in other little ways. A quicker native intelligence she had never seen. His nature was alert, foxlike, elusive; and his sense of humor was a strange thing. He was constantly picking up little differences between her life and speech and his at home. He heard somebody call " pants " trousers, for instance, and over that he had a fit of derisive laughter. Indeed, what amused her most was his perfect complacence with his way of life and thinking; his unquestioning faith that his way was the right way, and any other way justly a matter of surprise, comment and ridicule. It suggested to Anne parallelisms elsewhere, as circles widen, and helped her own breadth of view in judging him. What the boy had done to be in prison she did not know. She had not thought to ask her father; she could not ask the boy the first morning he came; and, after that, she thought she would rather not know, for his own sake and for the sake of his kinsman, Boone.

Meanwhile the days lengthened, and Anne took long drives in the slow twilights, sometimes with Marshall, but usually with Katherine Craig; and the constant cry of the mountaineer's nature for open air led Boone Stallard on long walks into the fields to keep his blood running and his brain clear. Often Anne, with Marshall or with Katherine, met the mountaineer miles from town, striding the road with his hat off; and sometimes, driving alone, she caught a glimpse of his big frame moving across Arnold's Wold in the late dusk. That was as close as she ever saw him; for resolutely he kept his distance from her, and the tractive force of novelty had its effect with Anne. She wanted to see the man again and to talk with him. It was a fact, frankly confessed to Katherine — to anybody who would not have misunderstood her. She was curious about his past, his purpose, his people. So overtaking Colton with the mountaineer one afternoon on the edge of town, she and Katherine took them both into the carriage and drove down the river and out through the Benson Hills. It was like crossing the border-line of her life and his when they passed a little cross-roads store. Several horses were hitched to the fence near by. Several men were whittling on the high stoop. More were pitching horseshoes up the dirt road, and at the blacksmith's shop beyond, three stalwart young fellows and a fat old farmer were playing marbles. Stallard smiled as though the scene were familiar. A little farther on was a two-roomed house, half of which was built of logs. At the wood-pile and leaning on his axe, was a tall, gaunt fellow, with a sunburnt blond beard, his trousers in his boots, and the brim of his slouched hat curved over his forehead. Farther still, a mile or more, they came upon a log cabin with a grape-vine over the door. An old woman, with a basket on one arm, was pushing through the rickety gate. She turned her face towards them as they passed, and peered as though she were straining her eyes through darkness.

"Howdy, mother?" said Stallard.

The old woman gave some quavering answer, and Stallard looked back once. It was the first time he had opened his lips, and the kindness of his voice touched Anne.

"Some people down in these hills are like your people, Stallard," said Colton. "I don't know whether they floated down the river, or whether it's because it's just hilly down here. They don't have as many curious words as you folks have; they don't have feuds; and they don't call the blue-grass the 'settlemints,' and us blue-grass people 'furriners,' but otherwise they are pretty much the same."

Several times Katherine, who sat with Stallard on the rear seat of the old-fashioned victoria, had tried to draw him out; and now Colton's purpose apparently was to start the mountaineer talking, but he only laughed good-naturedly at the differentiating characterization that Colton tossed off, and settled back into silence.

"It's all isolation," Colton went on; "that's what Reynolds was going to say the other night. Isolation arrests development, crystallizes character, makes a people deteriorate. That's his idea, and he says the Kentucky mountaineer has been the most isolated of all the Southern mountaineers—of whom, by-the-way, there are about three millions, with a territory as big as the German Empire. He has seen fringed hunting-shirts, moccasins, and coon-skin caps in the mountains at this late day. He swears that an old mountaineer once told him about the discovery of America by Columbus. Reynolds listened, solemn as an owl. The old chap called himself a 'citizen,' Reynolds a 'furriner,' and Columbus one of the 'outlandish.' He was a sort of patriarch in his district, a philosopher; he was the man who delivered the facts of progress to the people about him, and it never occurred to him that anybody as young as Reynolds might know about Columbus. The old fellow talked about the Mexican war as though it had been over about ten years, and when he got down to the Secession, well, he actually hitched his chair up to Reynolds's and dropped his voice to a whisper. 'Some folks had other idees,' he said, 'but hit was his pussonal opinion that *niggahs* was the cause of the war.' Think of it! And when Reynolds left, the old man followed him out to the fence: 'Stranger,' he said, 'I'd ruther you wouldn't say nothin' about what I been tellin' ye.' He was one of the few rebel sympathizers in that neighborhood, and he feared violence at that late day for talking too freely about the war. Reynolds claims that the mountaineers were loyal to the Union in '61 because they hadn't … o … .ie fight of 1776, and that these feuds ι.e the spent force of the late war. There were more slave-holders among the Kentucky mountaineers; for that reason, they were more evenly divided among themselves; the war issue became a personal one, and isolation kept them fighting. So you have to go back to the Revolution to understand the mountaineer, and you must give him a lonely century in which to deteriorate before you can judge him fairly. Consider his isolation, says Reynolds, and the wonder is not that he is so bad, but that he isn't worse."

Colton could imitate the dialect well, and Anne listened with amused interest. Stallard laughed and nodded affirmatively, but all the while his eyes were on the passing fields. They had turned off from the river now and through the hills into Anne's land — the blue-grass. Back towards the town was a soft haze; before them, all was clear and brilliant. They had left the locust blossoms dropping meaninglessly into the streets. Here in the fields, Nature was making ready for the days when she can sit with folded hands, brooding and happy over work that is all but done. The blue-grass was purpling into soft seas, that rocked as proudly in the wind as the heading wheat and barley and the young green oats, whose silver-gray would be the last passing sheen of the summer's glory. Already the rifled clover blossoms were drooping their heads as the gray spikes of timothy shot exultantly above them. Now and then, from the road-side, came the low, sweet, aimless plaint of a little brown songster, whose name Anne had never learned. Two kingbirds were chasing a crow towards a woodland. Out in the meadow, a starling was poised over his nesting mate, balancing against the breeze, and swearing fealty for one happy month by the crimson on his wings. Quail were calling from the wheat, and larks were wheeling and singing everywhere. Sturdy farm-houses of plain brick stood out here and there from the sunlit fields, and now and then an avenue of locusts gave sight of a portico with great pillars running two stories high. It was a scene of rich peace and plenty, and Stallard's interest was eager, but Anne noticed his face sadden. She remembered this afterwards, as she recalled other impressions of the drive, when she had a key to the meaning of them. Once only, when one of the mountaineer's questions to Colton showed how well he knew the country, could she ask him if he had not been to the blue-grass before.

"You went to the university, didn't you?" she said.

The careless query seemed almost to startle him. He turned quickly to her and, for the first time, looked straight into her eyes.

"Yes," he said, simply, and he seemed

to be waiting for another question that was on Anne's lips; but his look now brought back a sharp memory of his face on the night of the dinner, and made her shrink from the question before Colton and Katherine, as she knew she would shrink if she were with him alone. If he were the same, and if, as she suspected, he remembered her, why was he so palpably making of the matter such a mystery?

It was a short, swift ride, but nobody guessed the significance of it to the mountaineer. Only Anne noticed that when they turned from the gray haze settling over the blue-grass ahead of them, back to the smoke haze over the town, Stallard sank into a moodier silence still; and when they reached the darkening hills, something in his face assailed her once more with an unaccountable pity for him. They were passing the old woman's cabin at the time, and Anne's eyes followed his through the open door, where the old granny was bending over a fire, and the light showed the rude table set for the rude supper, and other hard details of the room. To her it was merely a passing picture etched by the light against a dark little ravine, but had she known the memories it brought to Stallard, she would have understood the sudden shadow in his face. The quick throb of her sympathy then made her shake off straightway what she chose to regard as a silly fear; and when they stopped at the Mansion, and Colton was climbing out, she said to Stallard, quite frankly:

"I wish you would come to see me. I want to know all about the mountains and the feuds—and everything."

Stallard did not answer at once, but looked at her so long and so searchingly that she began to flush, and Katherine, from sheer embarrassment, rose quickly to take Colton's outstretched hand, so little did the mountaineer seem at that moment to be aware of her presence or to care who might hear what he said.

"I'll tell you anything on earth you want to know—some day."

The tone of his voice made Colton start, and brought dead silence to the four.

Marshall was coming down the steps, and instinctively Anne covered her confusion with a look of dismay to Katherine; she had had an engagement with Marshall; she was getting back too late, and he would be angry. Seeing him, Stallard, who had stepped to the pavement, turned sharply from Anne, who was waiting for him to help her out, and held his eyes on Marshall until the latter was several paces down the street. It was a strange thing to do, and it mystified even Colton: but it was merely the mountaineer in him that made him keep his face with watchful suspicion on his enemy; it showed progress in the hostility between the two, and it was partly in answer to the half-contemptuous flash that Marshall gave Stallard, as he coldly lifted his hat.

VIII

But again Stallard did not come, and again Anne forgave him. He was exceptional; he was busy; he was shy—and he was not shy; there were a thousand things in addition to the one that was important: she became quite sure that he was avoiding her for some definite reason, and that bothered her a good deal. Once she met him for a moment on the steps of the Capitol and, with intentional lightness, she reminded him of his broken promise. That time he took her words with a seriousness not so deadly; and, thereafter, as the days went by, her fear abated and her interest grew.

Just now she was sitting on the old worn steps of the ancient Hannah mansion. The blue-grass was rich under the trees around her, the birds were singing as though love were going to live forever, and the soft air was like some comforting human presence. As she rose to start home, she saw Stallard emerge from the old wooden bridge, and she sat down again. The session was doubtless just over and he was going for a walk. He passed along the other side of the street without seeing her, and in a moment she rose again. She knew her motive when she hesitated at the gate and turned the same way, smiling indulgently at herself as she walked along, and, a little later, smiling at chance, which is sometimes genial, when she saw that she would meet Stallard where one road turns down the river and another winds up the hill. The mountaineer had been down one way; had changed his mind and was coming back. She stepped from the sidewalk to take the road up the hill, with her face turned to him to speak and expecting him to keep his course; but, without looking up and not hearing her light step, he turned, too, and they met in the middle of the road.

"Are we going the same way?" she asked, without calling him by name.

Surprise a mountaineer and you startle him. It is an inherited trait of people who live primitive lives among the hills and must be on the alert for an enemy. Instantly Stallard's hands were withdrawn from his pockets and a watchful light quickened in his eyes.

"Well," he said, "you skeered me!"

It was the slip of surprise, but Colton had made even vulgarisms like this tolerable for her. Much of the mountaineer's speech was simply obsolete elsewhere, he had explained. The mountaineer clung to old customs, old words, old pronunciations, because new ones had never reached him. Certain words were no more incorrect than certain customs were immoral. In the outer world, both were old-fashioned merely.

"I'm goin' up on the hill," he said, with a gesture. "Are you?"

"Yes," she said, simply, for in the fraction of time between his speech and hers she so made up her mind.

The smooth-beaten turnpike, shining like metal ahead of them, was canopied with interwoven branches and dappled with the sunlight that fell through them. Hill, tree, and the singing of birds were on the right hand, and the town lay under its haze of smoke to the left. It is against etiquette in the mountains for a young man and a young woman to stroll unchaperoned in the woods — a guardian seems necessary only for the extremes of civilization — and when Anne suggested turning aside to look for flowers, the mountaineer hesitated instinctively, and then, with a subtler thought, pushed open the little gate that swung from the body of an oak where she had stopped. The leaves in the woods were full, and the sunlight had the gold of autumn.

Stallard began drawing in his breath. "I always come up here when I'm homesick," he said. "It makes me think of the mountains — these hills. There's a mountain tree there, and there, and there's another," pointing out a lynn, a chestnut, a beech. "There are mountain birds up here, too"—a polyglot chat was chuckling. "Hear that? My father used to call that the 'plough-bird.' It goes up the trunk of a tree—Gee! Haw!—first to the right and then to the left; then it halts and clucks, just as though it wanted a steer to move on. When it gets to the branches, it drops down through the air as though it were hurt, and begins all over again. And this air"—drawing it into his great chest—"I can smell the roots of that sassafras. There's a spring up here, too. It's the only place where I can get a good drink of water."

It seemed volubility, so long a speech, and it gave Anne a surprise, as did the mountaineer's change of manner. He was quite easy and unconscious now, for he was with her alone, and he was in the woods, where he was at home. They were going up a path through a tangled thicket of undergrowth. A little stream of water tinkled down the ravine like a child prattling to itself, and tinkled dreamily on through dark shadows into the sunlight. A bluebird fluttered across it and, high above them, a cardinal drew a sinuous line of scarlet through the green gloom and dropped with a splutter of fire into a cool pool.

"Well," laughed Stallard, "he's in my spring." Somewhere out in the depths, just then, rose cool flutelike notes, as though satyrs were teaching young fauns to play on reeds. "That's another," said

Stallard, delightedly. "It's the first time I've heard him. I don't know what his name is."

"That's a wood-thrush," said Anne, stopping at the base of a tree and sinking down on a root. She had gathered only a few flowers, but she was tired.

Stallard stretched his long length in the grass below her. He was listening to the wood-thrush and, for the moment, he forgot her, or he had not learned that she let little pass unseen; for she was following his mood as it became thoughtful, reminiscent, and passed finally into the deep sadness she had noted on the drive. It was the second time she had ever seen his face relax from the fixed look that made it inscrutable as to all else except some dominant purpose. It had nothing of the dreaming quality of Marshall's pensive moods, it was not temperamental; it came from some definite, tangible source, for it got bitter and hard as the mood held him, even after the bird's gentle fluting ceased a moment and again came like an echo from a distant glade.

"I think you must have forgotten, haven't you?" she asked, again playfully, to divest the question, as well as the memory that it must bring to both, of especial significance.

He knew what she meant. "Oh no."

"Well, then, it's a good time to begin. I'm waiting." She was pulling a stalk of blue-grass from its casing, and Stallard turned to look full at her. "Why do you want to know?"

It was well that she was doing something, or the sudden question and the peculiar tone of it would have taken her off guard. As it was, there was no need for her eyelashes to lift until the stalk came loose. Then she raised its white base to her lips and bit it off quite calmly.

"You mustn't ask me reasons; you must never ask any woman reasons."

It was her first parry, and she saw that parrying with him was going to be difficult—his thrusts were so out of rule. He was looking at her in a blunt, penetrating way, and she did not lift her eyes until his face was turned again towards the faint piping of the thrush. She was not ready to enter that question with herself, much less with him.

"There ain't much to tell," he was saying, slowly. "I live at the head-waters of the Cumberland, where the mountains are purty steep. A neighbor of mine fell out of his own corn-field once and broke his neck. I went to school in a log-house for three months in winter for three years, working and studying at home between times. I stopped then because I knew more than the man who was teaching the school. I made enough money, logging, to get to the Bible college at Lexington. I soon found out I wasn't called to be a preacher, so I went over into the College of Arts. I worked in the professors' gardens; I did my own cooking—anything—everything. It took me six years, but I got through. I went back home and I taught school and I studied law. Then I practised at my country-seat until I ran for the Legislature. That's all."

That was all. It was a plain record of plain facts, and Anne knew not half the tale of hardship that was left untold; what the bitter, patient fight with the hard conditions of his birth had been, she could not even guess.

"Yes, it was a purty hard row," he added, simply, as though he were following her thoughts; "but I'd hoe it over again if it had to be done—for one reason, anyhow—because I can do more for my people. But for that I think, sometimes, that I wouldn't, if I were back at the beginning, knowing what I know now, and had my choice. It nearly cost me my religion, and it left me hung midway between heaven and hell. Then I've learned to rebel against what I can't escape, and to value what I can never get."

Stallard's face settled back into reverie, and there was a long silence—so little was there that Anne could say. She was curious to know definitely what he meant; he had opened the way, whether purposely or not, for her to ask, but she swerved from the question, and asked quite another:

"Where did you learn to speak?"

Stallard laughed. "I never learned. It's natural, what there is of it. I used to pray in meetin's when I was a boy. Then I used to speak in college. I never could write a speech—I have to talk offhand. That's the way I made my valedictory." He laughed again, and Anne gave a little cry of surprise.

"Yes, I remember; that was you, too."

"You heard of that?" he asked.

"Who didn't?" was her answer, and Stallard's face shone.

It was epoch-making in the history of valedictories at the old university — that speech; and the pathos of it was unintentional and quite unconscious. A big, rough, manly countryman had stepped out and spoken from a slip of notes in his hand. He was not sorry to go, he said, calmly. He had worked hard; he had asked no favors, incurred no obligation. He had come as rough material; he had paid for the privilege of being planed down. The professors were paid to plane him down. He had tried to do his duty; he believed they had done theirs. He had no personal gratitude to express to anybody. Nor had he any pathetic farewell to make to the people of the town. He had received no hospitality at their hands. He had been under hardly a single roof outside the campus. He knew the face of hardly a woman before him. He had not a word of complaint or blame. There was no reason why the facts of his college life should have been otherwise; only they were not. The honor of the valedictory had not been conferred on him by his classmates, nor by the professors, nor by the people of the town. He had won that, working for something else. He knew what the valedictorian was expected to do. He had been listening to valedictories for six years. He could not doubt the sincerity of his predecessors, but he must tell what was the truth for him; and doing that, he could not follow them. He had his little memories, associations, friendships; they were few, but they were too sacred for him to bid them farewell from that platform. He had come an alien—an alien he was going away. And he was glad to go—to get to other work. He would have liked to give them high-wrought sentiment, shining metaphors; to wring them with the agony of farewell into tears even; but he had to tell the truth. The truth was what he had told, and more to tell there was not. So speaking, he sat down.

The good old president sat through it bewildered and pained. The professor of English looked mad. The bluff old professor of Greek was laughing in his eyes and under his right hand, which covered his mouth. The dean of the Bible college, who had labored to save Stallard's soul from perdition and his powers for the church, was openly resentful and hurt; while the little man who helped experiments in the laboratory was laughing in his sleeve at them all. The same variety of results was perceptible in the house. Only the editor of the town paper and a few scattered bold spirits broke into applause, but the hall hummed just the same, and the speaker was the man of the day.

"Why, I'm not a patchin' to Sherd Raines," Stallard went on—"the fellow I roomed with at college. He and I made a bargain when I found out I wasn't 'called.'

He said he'd teach the folks at home religion if I'd teach 'em law."

"What are you going to do—what do you want to do?"

"My best, always, and let the rest go. I'm a fatalist, I reckon, as I found out when I studied moral philosophy. I take what comes, if it is better than what I have. I have my wishes, my hopes, even a definite ambition; but I sha'n't risk wrecking my life on it, especially when what I most wish for I knew nothing of until it was too late to acquire it, if it was not denied me even to acquire it, when I was born."

He pulled down the brim of his hat and looked away. Some instinct, some fear held her back from asking just what he meant, and she watched him, greatly puzzled. She was sure now that his was the strongest face she had ever seen; and his history was as plain in it as it was in his words. There was not a line about brow, nose, mouth, or chin that was not chiselled into force of character, force of purpose. If there was a hint of contradiction in his make-up, it was too fine for her vision, keen as that was. It was the flawlessness in this one bulwark of strength that had drawn her and made her fear. She shrank from his eyes when he turned all at once to her; there was a light in them that was not pleasant.

"I wonder if you could guess what turned me away from religion to law?"

He pointed to the yellow dome of the Capitol through a rift in the trees, and she knew the half of what he meant—that he meant Marshall. "I was in the Bible college, and the first Commencement I ever saw was his. I heard his speech; he had the salutatory; and I was right under him, looking up into his face. He spoke over my head and never saw me. It was Kentucky for the Kentuckians—his speech —and he didn't let us mountain folks in at all. I couldn't catch his eye when he spoke of my people as he did down there in the House the other day. I knew him the moment he got up, and I felt just as I did away back in college. It's kind o' like a storm down in the mountains when the river is high. I can hear the wind crashing the big trees together and the water roar. Lightning just seems to flash in front of my eyes, and I can hear the thunder—I tell you, I can *hear* it. That's the way it is below." Stallard moved his hand to and fro, as though he were on some peak and the elements were raging under him. " I'm up above somehow "— tapping his forehead—" an' I seem to have the strength of them all right here "— stretching out his right hand and gripping it—" and I know that what I want to do then, is done. I know that now. That's the way I felt after his speech in college that day when the band crashed in from the gallery; and the people clapped their hands; and the ushers, with flowers in their button-holes and their canes wrapped in red and white and blue ribbons, carried him up notes and flowers; and everybody talked and smiled and nodded; and he sitting upon the platform, looking red and proud and happy. I must have been a great fool, for I could hardly keep from getting up right then and shouting out, 'Brother, you ain't the only man as can do that'; and, thank God, the time did come at last."

Stallard stopped short, seeing Anne's pained and helpless face. He had spoken quietly, but a zigzag streak of red had run up and down each side of his face, and he had had to stop, now and then, in the hesitancy that with him meant violent emotion. Anne did not speak again until she saw that he had himself in hand once more.

"I was there that day," she found herself saying, partly that he might not think she was shifting too suddenly away from the theme.

"Yes," he said, quickly. "I saw you. You dropped your umbrella, and you waited for me to pick it up—out on the steps."

He spoke calmly and as though with a quickly made resolution, and the girl started and listened—surprised, perplexed, and watching with the strength of her soul in her eyes.

He knew then; he had known all along; why— And then, because the woman in her could not help herself:

"Why didn't you pick it up?"

He did not answer. If he even heard her, he did not show it; he was going on as though she were asking him quite another question:

"Yes, my people live down in the mountains; they have been there a hundred years. My father is dead. My mother is at home, and one married sister, whose worthless husband was killed in the feud. My sister is hardly older than you, I imagine, and yet she looks old enough to be your mother. She has four children, and she has worked in the fields"—Anne shrank, and he saw—"not before her marriage, mind you, nor since her husband's death. Let me see your hand."

She held it out with the sensation of obeying an unspoken command. He looked at it intently—the pink nails, long white fingers, the threadlike veins in the round wrist—but he did not touch it.

"Her's is like mine," he said, turning over his broad palm. "It's hard and rough and sunburnt; and his looks as soft as yours, almost."

"Haven't you any brothers?" she asked, quickly, to turn him away from the dangerous theme; and then she trembled at her own question, for Stallard started visibly and did not reply at once.

"Two," he said, at last. "One is at

home—he is a half-brother; and the other"—his tone got harsh, he rose suddenly to his feet, and answered with his back to her: "He's in jail."

"Oh—" It was a swift cry of pain, of apology, and it was enough.

The mountaineer had turned full upon her. "I want you to know—everything. My mother can't write her own name. My sister barely can. My father made his mark, though his father's father wrote a better hand than I do—an old deed shows that. My mother is rough, ignorant, not a lady as you would say, though she is the best woman I know on earth. They are all mountaineers, ignorant mountaineers; as Marshall would call them," he added, bitterly, "'pore white trash.' My brother is in jail, as he deserves to be."

And then Stallard went on to tell about that brother; how he had done all he could to keep him from the evil to which, as a boy even, he seemed irresistibly drawn.

How he had kept aloof from the feud in which his brother had taken an active part; how the latter had sunk lower and lower until just punishment had caught him at last. He himself was like his mother; his brother was more violent and had less restraint, like his father; that was the difference between the two. The turn of a hand and each might have had the other's fate. That was the way of chance.

"My mother's people came from eastern Virginia, like yours. They owned slaves, like yours. Yours came here; mine stayed in the wilderness. You kept your level; we went down; through no virtue of yours, no fault of ours. It was fate. I think of Marshall and you, and of my sister and me. You were born so; we were born so. For that reason what's yours without the asking is not ours at any cost —not now. If there's a worse blow in the face of a man who does the best with what comes to him than to learn the value

of what he can never get, I hope it may
be spared me. To be willing to do anything, deny everything, and to know that
neither the one nor the other can ever
wholly count, that—" Stallard waved
his hand, through sheer inability to go on.
Neither knew the full and personal significance of what he said, but through it
all the girl sat pained and mute, touched
too deep down for tears. She kept silent,
even when they rose and went down the
path again, though Stallard, with unsus-
pected delicacy, turned his talk again to
the birds and trees. Only when he reached the gate at the oak did he strike the
chord again.

"I didn't pick it up," he said, "because
I didn't even see it until you started down
for it yourself. I was looking at you. I
had followed you out of the hall to see
you again. And no day has passed since,
no hour hardly, that I have not seen you
looking at me with a smile, just as you

looked then. It is not so strange. You want to see the best in the world, know the best, be the best. Don't you think it would be easy, then, for you to remember your first vision of what you realized was the best? Especially when, thereafter, you are shut off for years from all that is best? I couldn't have forgotten you, if I had tried. Sometimes I have tried. But for you, after all, I might not have gone on. I might be living in a log cabin in the mountains, and tied there, with a wife and children, forever—and it might be the better for me if I were. But you helped open to me the world against which I am still knocking for entrance— you and he — see what I owe you — yes, and *him*, too. And you are helping open it now — the same world which, I am afraid, is barred me as heaven is, for, without cowardice or disloyalty, I can never escape my own. I didn't know you at first—" He stopped, holding her eyes with his, so that, in the moment of silence, she felt weak and afraid and was glad when he went on. "You are not as lovely as I thought you were"—she could not smile even to herself at his honesty—"and no wonder. Your face has always been the face of something unearthly to me, and now I see the human. I didn't know you until you smiled at me the other night, when you were singing, and I never quite know you as the same, unless you look as you looked then—as you look now," he added, for Anne was smiling faintly. Stallard's voice was so gentle and kind, and it was all so strange. He never dreamed that she could doubt a scintilla of what he said; nor did she, strange as it all was.

Stallard had opened the gate and, mountaineerlike, had gone through first and was holding it open for her. As she passed through she paused, lifting her eyes suddenly to his.

"I saw you that day—I remember, too." The words rose impulsively to her half-open lips, but some vague dread held them back.

The sun was cutting like a great red scimitar down through a shadowed hill in the west. Arnold's Wold was already in dusk. A cloud of smoke was rising above the prison, and the Catholic cross rose whitely through it, as though swung down from above. There was still a purple glow edging the clouds in the east, and the marble on the hill caught the last light sadly. To Anne the past hour was already taking the misty shape of a dream—into such a melodrama had the facts of both their lives in that hour been cast, in spite of the simple, open story Stallard had told. In no way had he made an appeal to her pity, or to her sympathies; for that reason, he had both wholly. Outwardly now, as they went down the hill, he was ironlike once more;

but there was a softer ring in his voice when he spoke, and a new tone of understanding. On the old bridge he stopped—looking up stream. A long raft of logs was floating down the river towards them.

"That's the way I came down to go to college," he said, smiling. "I walked from here to Lexington."

A mountaineer was standing at the huge stern oar, motionless. As the end of the raft swung under them they could hear him singing; and, still smiling, Stallard bent his head to listen.

"I've got a gal at the head of the holler,
Heh-o-dee-um-dee-eedle-dahdy-dee!"

And then he swept the big paddle through the water. Anne, too, smiled; it was the song the young trusty sang in the garden. Stallard bent lower and sang back.

"She won't come, an' I won't foller."

The fellow looked quickly up, gave a "hooray," and, with a wave of his hat, sent the refrain up with a hearty swing,

"Heh-o-dee-um-dee-eedle-dahdy-dee!"

"He doesn't know me, but he knows that I know where he's from," said Stallard. "I used to go over to the Kentucky River and bring logs down that way. We'd tie up to the bank, and then we'd all go up the middle of the street single file. We didn't know what the sidewalks (hearth-stones I remember old Tom Perkins used to call them) were for. We went back part of the way on the train, and we climbed through the windows, not knowing where the doors were. We called the cars 'boxes.' One fellow climbed over the fence to his boarding-house, never having seen a gate. I didn't much expect in those days that I'd be walking along here some day as a member of the 'Legislatur,' as we say, and with the Governor's daughter, and she the same—"

He stopped suddenly and stiffened. At the end of the bridge was Marshall, who stepped aside with unnecessary ceremony and, lifting his hat, bowed with elaborate courtesy. Not until he saw Anne's flush, did Stallard notice that Marshall was almost staggering. At the steps of the Mansion, Anne left her hand in Stallard's as though she would say one of the thousand things that were on her tongue; but her lip quivered, and that was all.

IX

The session drew to a close. Several times, Anne met Stallard in the street and he spoke merely, lifting his hat now, and passed on. She had asked him once if he expected to come back the following year. His answer was that he didn't know; he would come, if he were sent; but that he did not mean to turn his hand over for a renomination. Considering the extraordinary coincidence of their lives, the extraordinary disclosure which linked the present with the past, and the possible fact that, in a few weeks, he might see her for the last time, his course now was inexplicable. He kept to his seclusion rigidly. She could not believe that his interest in her was impersonal, that he regarded her as merely a spiritual embodiment of certain conditions that were denied him at birth, that he wanted to attain, and which he believed were beyond him altogether. It was only after much thought that the truth flashed and seared her to the heart. He saw the gulf between them. He believed she thought it impassable, and, with his strong sense and sure insight, he, too, saw that it was. He was too proud to make an effort to bridge the gulf — too loyal to his own people to cross it alone, if he could. He would walk with them on his own side; and with this resolution he must do as he was doing. She liked his pride, and, for that reason, the hard conditions on which he must uphold it wrung her the more with pity.

Marshall, too, she rarely saw, and she knew the reason. He had not been to the Mansion since the night she and Stallard met him at the bridge. What she heard of the two men in the House kept her continually uneasy: for no matter came up there in which Stallard and Marshall did not antagonize each other, and Marshall said sharp things which, from Stallard's lips, Anne knew, would bring about trouble.

To many, Marshall's bitterness seemed unreasonable, but perhaps there was only one other person, than Colton, who so much as suspected that his hostility was not altogether political: that was Katherine Craig. She saw the inner play of his mind, of which Marshall himself was hardly conscious, and she sensibly kept it to herself. Hitherto, Marshall had met his rivals chivalrously, as he would have met them, man to man, in any conflict— as he would have met Stallard, had the mountaineer been a gentleman. He always said that he had never known jealousy—that a common admiration was to him a link of sympathy rather than a cause of hate — and to his rivals he was especially courteous. A foreign lover got from no one a more hospitable welcome than from Marshall; but, with Stallard, it was different. The mountaineer had shown himself a boor by exposing his enmity before ladies and in a drawing-room. War was declared between the two before he had even looked upon Stallard as a possible rival. Not that he seriously saw him in that light yet—but, still, he was far too keen not to feel the hold the mountaineer had; and it vexed him with Anne, to whom he dared not open his lips, and gave a surprising force to his feeling against Stallard. The mountaineer had power as an orator. But one thing appealed to the girl more—political honor—and that, he knew, Anne believed the mountaineer irresistibly bound to achieve. These would win her admiration, her interest, her respect; and that much Stallard already had —yes, he confessed quickly, and more. The mountaineer was, in her eyes, a man with a people behind him — a people who had drifted back towards barbarism through no fault of their own. They were kindred in distress, and his mission was to aid, to uplift. Moreover, he was new to her in all ways, and he had not dropped, like the others, at once to her feet. Such points of favor, Marshall counted, could never win Stallard more than deep interest, deep friendship, perhaps. The idea of love would be as repugnant to her, he believed, as it was to him. Intellectually, she was quite democratic, and she avowed democracy, but in her exactions and deepest feelings she was aristocrat to her heart's core. Thus far, Marshall could go; thus far, he went. But how Stallard's personal history, his early upward fight, his frank facing of the facts of his birth, his just bitterness that fate should draw the deadline for one man who wanted to cross it and suffer another to be born on the other side and care nothing for the advantage;

how the secret inner sorrow that his brother had put upon him stirred her passionate pity—of all that he knew nothing, or he might have been uneasy indeed.

Anne found herself in a curious maze. This brother of Stallard's was, of course, Buck, the young trusty; that was doubtless what he had yet to tell her. Criminals, after conviction, were sent to the penitentiary from all parts of the State; she knew that, but she did not know that moonshiners were not; and in some way she had come to believe that the young trusty's crime was "moonshining," which she had come to regard, through Buck's testimony and Colton's strictures on the revenue service, with much tolerance and a good deal of sympathy.

"It wasn't no harm once," Buck argued. "Ever'body made liquor—some fellers was jus' born to it. An' say, s'posin' you had a field o' corn in some deep hollow. You can't tote hit out an', if you did, you couldn't sell nary a grain. An' s'posin' you had a big family an' you jus' had to have somep'n to eat—coffee an' sweetenin' an sech. Whar you git the money? Thar's the corn an' that's all. Well, the corn is yourn, hain't it? Yes. Well, you can do whut you please with what's yourn, can't ye? You can put that corn in a pile an' burn hit if you wants to, can't ye? You can give hit away? Well, the only way you can git money fer that corn is to build ye a still an' turn hit into moonshine an' carry hit over into Virginny an' sell hit. An' I'd jus' like to know what right the Gover'mint—whut all our folks fit fer—has to step up, all of a sudden, an' say: 'Here, gimme some o' the money you got fer that corn o' yourn, or go to jail.'"

This was the boy's tale, and she forgave much to sincerity of motive no matter how mistaken it might be, and she had quite accustomed herself to thinking of him as the victim of circumstances and of a misdemeanor that was not in itself criminal. Thinking that, she had allowed her interest in him to deepen unreservedly; she had suffered him much liberty of speech; and now, Stallard had hinted at something in his brother as dark as crime could be: so that she was unsmiling the next time Buck came to work, but full of pity, as she watched him under a newspaper with which she shaded her eyes from the sun. Was it possible that this brightfaced lad, with his careless laughter and his easy chatter, had human blood on his hands?

"Hit's this way, Miz Anne," he was saying. "One o' them wars jus' knocks the fun out'n ever'thing. Somebody gives a party. Thar's Keatons thar, an' thar's Stallards thar. Purty soon thar's a row, an' the party is busted up. Folks is afeerd now to have parties. Sometimes a Stallard and a Keaton is a-courtin' the same gal, an' sometimes they both goes to see her the same night. Commonly, they makes the gal say which one she likes best, an' t'other one takes his foot in his hand an' lights fer home; but I knowed a case once whar the gal said she jus' didn't plumb know which."

The boy was wily as a fox; he stopped there. Something was wrong that morning—he saw it in Anne's face—and he was trying to get her interested.

"What happened then?" she asked, partly because she wanted to know, partly because he was waiting for the question.

"Well, they jus' stepped out'n doors an' fit. An' when Jim Stallard was a-gittin' the best o' Tom Keaton, the gal gits to cryin'; an' when Jim gits him down, she runs up an' pulls Jim off by his ha'r; an' Jim says the next time he fights fer a gal he wants to be the feller what's licked."

The girl laughed, when she felt close to

tears. Once she thought of asking him outright if he were a brother to Boone Stallard, but it was no longer possible; when the mountaineer wanted her to know, he would himself tell: and Anne went in-doors, much troubled.

That day, to her distress, all her doubt was dissolved.

In the afternoon she took some friends of her father through the prison. Passing through the dust-cloud of a room in which prisoners were making laths, her eyes caught the face and shape of a convict who was running a thin plank through one of the circular saws. The jaw of the face was square and strong; the cheek towards her was sunken as though by a bullet or a knife thrust; and, while she looked at him, the man, as though to answer her gaze, lifted his dusty brows, and the cold, evil eyes under them met hers and, dropping at once back to his work, left her shuddering.

Almost unconsciously she touched the warden's arm.

"Who is that man?"

The convict fell into a violent fit of coughing as she spoke, and, when the warden turned, Buck the trusty was nodding brightly to her, side by side with the man she meant.

"Oh, his name's Stallard—from down in the mountains—one of those feuds—murder. He's a pretty bad fellow; everybody asks about him. He's got a brother in the Legislature," he added to another of the party; but Anne heard him, and was sunk in such sudden wretchedness that she did not repeat her question. She felt her pity deepening for Stallard as she walked home, and when she went to her room that night, she was seeking palliation for the young trusty. It was hard to believe that he was evil in soul—he was so light-hearted, open, frank, and humorously curious. She found herself going back to the time when men exacted a blood penalty for a slain kinsman. She recalled the boys words:

"S'posin' somebody was to shoot down your brother, an' the law wouldn't tech him — not couldn't, now, mind ye — *wouldn't*. What would you do? What would any feller do?"

Then she faced the question; what, under such circumstances, would her own father do? She would learn the details before she judged the boy. No, she must not do even that; Stallard would tell her these when he wanted her to know. No; she— The thread was snapped there. Why was she trying to defend this boy? For his own sake, or through her pity of Stallard? Had the lad appealed to her on his own account? Yes, but, ah!—and just there the white hands slipped from the bright hair they had been loosening, and Anne sank into a chair by the window, looking out with startled eyes into the June night. When she went to bed, she lay there sleepless and a little frightened. She could not put one image outside her vision: now and then, in her half-conscious dreams, the young trusty would displace it; now and then, Marshall; oftenest of the three, the convict with the sunken cheek: but it always swung back before her closed eyes in the darkness, fixed, calm, inscrutable—the face of Stallard, the mountaineer.

X

She did not go down to breakfast next morning. She stayed abed and, early in the afternoon, Katherine Craig came with disturbing news. Down in the mountains, Colton had told her, Mace Keaton was at his deviltry again. He had elected himself sheriff, and had suffered a Stallard to be shot down within sight of him and had not raised his hand. Both parties were once more armed and organized, and the Keatons had taken to "the brush." The judge who had gone to the county-seat to hold court had been driven from town. Any day there might be a general conflict.

Elsewhere, Katherine had heard more. Marshall meant to bring up that day his old bill to disrupt the county. He would be bitter; and lately Stallard's patience, it was said, was being worn to an edge. Trouble was feared.

About that time, in the House, Marshall was rising to his feet. He repeated all he had said and more—bitterly. He addressed himself straight to the gentleman from Roland. Could he deny such and such, and such and such? And Stallard had to sit through it all, white and silent, for Marshall, drinking as he was, took care to state only facts. Still, the spirit of his talk was vindictive. It looked as though he wanted to bring about a mortal quarrel, and Colton, who was watching the mountaineer's face, believed it was going to come. The ticking of the big clock could be heard when the mountaineer rose, but there was no answering invective. Not once did Stallard's tone rise above the level of quiet conversation. He was pale and his eyes were bright, but in no other way did he show unusual emotion. The facts were as the gentleman had stated. He had said much; he had implied a good deal—that was irrelevant and unnecessary. It was not the place where those things should be said, discussed, or answered. The gentleman seemed to hold him personally responsible for the lawlessness of his people. Very well, he would accept and bear the responsibility, and he pledged that body that he personally would see that law and order, in the end, prevailed.

The pressure of affairs—for the term was growing short—and Marshall's manner and condition were already seriously against his bill. Stallard's temperate words defeated it, and Marshall's face, flushed as it was, paled a little. He was standing in the lobby, when Colton came out, and a friend had him by the arm and was trying to lead him away. He tried to break loose when Stallard appeared, and Colton saw the mountaineer's mouth tighten and a dangerous light leap from his eyes as he stopped still and waited. Another friend caught Marshall's arm, and Stallard walked on as though he had seen nothing. But he went on with a quickening step over the bridge, and he walked the hills till dark. The animal in him that he had been slowly netting with such care was straining at its cords now. It is never securely bound in a nature as close to earth as Stallard's was; and nothing will make it restive like the kindly eyes and voice of a woman and a rival claim for them. It had turned with leaping fury in Stallard and made him primeval again. Marshall was not fooling him. He knew the true reason for the bitter hostility of that day. Marshall feared him without, as well as within, the legislative chamber. The mountaineer had no traditions of chivalry to hold him in check; and he went on stripping himself, stripping Marshall, until soul to soul the two faced in a mortal fight for mastery. And could Anne have seen his face when the moon rose on it out in the fields, she would have heard her heart beat. Had Marshall been face to face with him in fact, as he was in mind, the mountaineer would have killed him and gone striding on through the fragrant dusk, an exultant savage.

It was late when he got back, but the strain of his heart and his brain was eased; and the inner structure that a strong soul builds on religion first, and then on a love of law that is born of a love of people who are in need of restraint, was firm within him again. He got to his room and to his books with the tempest in him calm, and the old, old resolution freshly made to run his course, as he had started, to the end.

He had a hard time with his law that night. Things were always passing between his eyes and the page that blurred the print; and he was glad when the hour came for the walk that was a nightly custom with him after his task was done. Not that he needed exercise that night; but the walk always took him past Anne Bruce's house, and it was for that sole reason that he went now. There was a dim light in the hallway, but the parlor was dark, and so was Anne's room, which he had come to know from seeing her at her window, half screened by maple leaves. As he passed the rear of the hotel beyond, music started through the open windows above him, and he remembered that the last hop of the season was going on that night. Anne was doubtless there — and Marshall. Farther up the street, an unusual clinking of glasses came from behind a pair of green shutters, and there was an unusual stir on the portico and in the hallway of the hotel. At the top of the steps stood Colton in evening dress, mopping his face with a handkerchief. Stallard had declined to go when Colton urged him that morning, but he let himself be dragged up-stairs now to the door of the ballroom, and there he halted and stood —a grave, unsmiling statue—looking on. He had never seen waltzing before, and, while he watched, his mind was on a dance at home—a log cabin, a fiddle and a banjo, a puncheon floor, and men in jeans and cowhide boots swinging girls in linsey under low, blackened rafters and through the wavering light of a tallow dip. And the prompting: "Balance all! Swing yer pardners! Cage the bird! Grand right an' *wrong!* Fust lady to the right—*cheat* an' swing." What a contrast! Katherine smiled at him as she whirled past, and, through the dancers, he saw Anne at the other end of the room and, near her, Marshall—dark, grave, and faultless in dress and bearing. Already she was gathering up her wraps and, when the dance was over, she was moving on

Marshall's arm towards the door. She was going home, and Stallard shrank back that she might not see him. As she passed, he saw that she was biting her lip under a forced smile, and Marshall was frowning darkly. Something was wrong between the two, and it pleased him savagely.

He did not wait long after they were gone; the brilliant scene thrust him farther and farther from Anne. Even to his eyes she was marked from every other woman in the room by her simple presence, which seemed out of keeping with the rush and whirl of the place. And if she were out of place in these lights, with this music, among these dainty things in white—how would she seem at home? The thought stung him, as he turned away; it added to his store of bitterness, but it helped make his purpose firm.

The Mansion was only two blocks distant, and straight on Stallard's way home.

The door opened just as he was passing by on the other side of the street, and, having stopped unconsciously in the thick shadow of a maple, he feared to move on. Marshall came out, with his hat in his hand, and Anne stood in the door. It was after midnight, and the street was still. Marshall turned and began talking in a low tone and rapidly. Anne leaned in the doorway, with her hands behind her. Her attitude was indifferent and her face looked hard. She made no answer as Marshall moved down the steps, and, for the second time that day, an exultant fire ran through him. She stood a little while just as Marshall had left her, and then she came to the edge of the porch, looking across through the darkness where he was hungrily watching her. Her eyes seemed almost to be on him, as he stood uneasy and noiseless, but she turned and closed the door. He saw the light in the drawing-room and in the hall go out and, a moment later, another appear up-stairs; then her face through the leaves at the window and one hand reaching up for the curtain; and he stayed on, just to see her shadow pass now and then, till the room was dark.

He started for his room then, little reckoning how the girl lay looking with sleepless eyes into the darkness above her, mystified, perplexed, distressed. It was the first time Marshall had been to the Mansion for a long while, and they had had the worst of their many quarrels. She had heard of the trouble in the House fully, and her sympathies sided resistlessly with Stallard. Marshall *was* wrong, she tried to argue; it was a matter of justice, she said—as though justice guided a woman's sympathies, she thought, before the words had quite left her lips. Still, she had spoken as though Stallard were a stranger to both, and Marshall, with one reckless word, had made the matter personal. Then was she very plain with him. She rarely tried to hide the truth, even when there was no need for it to be known; for she was fearless of criticism and especially, just now, of his —for she thought him bitter and unjust. So, in her defence of the mountaineer, she indirectly laid bare her interest in him, and Marshall was startled. She feared that, in the heat of the moment, she had put that interest too strong; and she herself was startled to realize how little she had fallen short of the truth.

A revolution took place that night. Grown reckless at last, Anne faced fact after fact, extraordinary as each was, and finally went to troubled sleep, ceasing to question.

XI

It was well for the three that the session came to a quick end. Marshall went to his farm; Stallard to the mountains; Anne stayed on at the capital: the summer came and gave the three time to think.

Anne saw the leaves grow full, the hills round with beauty, and the flowers go. When the trees got dusty and the hot days came, she too went home. She saw nothing of Marshall; she heard nothing, and she was not surprised; for she knew his moods and his ways, she thought, beyond the chance of error. Nobody saw Marshall during those days; for he stayed at home, passing his own test of fire. Anne had cut his pride to the quick. The mountaineer had started with nothing, and had accomplished all that human effort could; while he, wanting nothing, had done only what his birth and station had impelled him to do: that was the blunt burden of the contrast that he had drawn on himself from Anne. In other and plainer words, he was little more than a machine, run by the momentum of forces that were prenatal. He deserved little credit for what he had done, and great censure for not having done more. That was the final courageous interpretation he gave her words, and it was not long before his self-searching honesty began to tell him that it was all true. His humiliation was bitter, but his hurt pride was turned into a power for good, and started a change in him that nothing else had ever been able to effect; for it forged and edged a purpose—started him on a course of grim self-denial and turned him to work.

THE KENTUCKIANS

A century back, new life was put into the lazy Virginia blood that fought its way over the Cumberland and along the Wilderness Road to the interior; it needed only antagonism then to give it new strength, and the vigor of that pioneer effort is far from spent. It is the bedrock of the Kentuckian's character to-day, and a shaft, sunk through his easy good-humor, rarely fails to rest on it at last. That far down, the differences between Marshall and Stallard practically ceased; down there, they would meet as granite meets granite, when a great test should come. But now, thanks to the guidance, since, of an unseen Hand, the mountaineer must fight away from the earth for strength, as Marshall, for help, must fight back to it: and the love of the same woman was the motive power that led them opposite ways.

They were long days that summer, and days of gain to both, but the Hand still bore with unequal weight on the mountaineer. Marshall saw his blue-grass stripped and stored, the grain harvested, the corn turn yellow for the knife. With the first crisp touch of frost, he was busy in the hemp-fields. Then came the brooding days of autumn, the gentle, pensive haze of Indian-summer, and the drowsy rest of nature filled his mother's heart and brought to his turbulent spirit an unguessed measure of peace.

Not a word came from the mountaineer. His mountains had swallowed him, as they swallow everything that passes their blue summits. Once Anne saw in a newspaper that the leaders in the Keaton-Stallard feud had met, shaken hands, and signed a truce; and that Boone Stallard had brought the reconciliation about. It was the one fact that she heard of him through the autumn, and she thought of him a good deal; for she was living alone; she had much time for speculations and dreams: and, moreover, the way of chance is strange. Had Stallard been an acute student of woman's nature, had he given years of study to Anne Bruce's heart and brain, and then have deliberately chosen the way to reach both, it is doubtful whether he could have picked a better part or have played it with better skill. To show his secret with every act and look, and but once—and barely then—with a spoken word; to trouble her with no exactions; to give all, in a word, and ask nothing; to be strong—so strong as to make her feel, with a vague dissatisfaction, that there was in him something stronger even than his love for her, and then to pass out of her life as silently as he came into it—to pass on and out of life altogether for aught she knew—there was hardly a detail left undone. For she read, later, that the truce was broken once more; she saw Buck Stallard's name among the prisoners whose time was done, and that surprised her and gave her great relief; that his crime was complicity in a feud — not murder — and that perplexed her and made her wonder. Then came news of a fight in which Buck had taken part and two Stallards were killed. One of them might have been Boone. Any other than he would have sent her word, if he were alive. Silence in another man would have been inexplicable — it meant nothing in Stallard. He had never so much as said that he was coming back; he had said, indeed, that he would not turn over his hand for the chance to return. He had said that — and yet he loved her: he had loved no other; his love, born years ago with a look, had suffered no change, no displacement: all this he had given her to understand as plainly as he could have put it into words. She would have smiled at such a tale in another man, and yet she hardly wondered at it in Stallard: she simply thought it strange that fate had made it so. Now he was gone—gone for good, as far as she knew. It would have been beyond reason in another man—it meant nothing in an inscrutable enigma like him. He was dead, even, as far as she knew; he might be and she not know; for once she had gone so far as to write Colton, who, too, had heard not a word. So, day by day, wondering, fearing, thinking—more than was good for her, good as it all was for Stallard's place in her heart—Anne had to wait and be patient till Christmas should come and the new year, when the session would open again. Then she would know, and not till then.

One thing only was there for her to know that summer, that would have distressed her less than news of his death, and that was the storm and stress of his life. He had told Anne the truth. He had gone home with the resolution not to lift hand or foot to secure his nomination.

Apparently no move was necessary; for, by the terms of the truce, Mace Keaton had left the mountains for a year, to give the heated blood of both factions time to cool; and, without Mace, there was no man to oppose him. So Boone Stallard gathered his mother's thin corn in peace, as did other Stallards and Keatons their corn, and it was the first summer in many years that many of either name had worked in the fields, without a rifle close at hand and the fear of an enemy lurking near in ambush. It was a time of inner tumult to the mountaineer, for it was an old story retold now—his coming back home, his revulsion from its narrow life; the rough talk of his friends in the presence of their daughters and wives; the rustic uncouthness of the young women; the painful pity that attacked him when he newly realized the hard lot of his mother and sister, whose unconsciousness made the pathos of it the more piteous;

to know how helpless he was to aid them in more than the simple needs of existence; how beyond him to broaden or uplift them, so crystallized were they in the way of life that had been moulded for them so long. Contrast—it was all bitter, hopeless contrast, when he saw his mother in the cabin at night with her pipe; his sister with hers, now; the neighbors drifting in with hats on, and barefooted sometimes—men and women; the talk—it struck him now with ludicrous inconsistency—of homicide and the Bible, the last killing and the doctrine of original sin—from the same lips, with hardly a breath to bridge the chasm between. Even in his early days, a sullen rebellion against the chains of birth would break loose within him; and now, with Anne's face always looking from water, mist, and moonlight, the rebellion was fierce; and half-crazed sometimes, he would start up the mountain, after his work was done, and climb until there was no leaf between him and the stars. There he would have it out with his own soul, and with the wide heaven that had put him where he was and did not chain him there. And there his strong courage upheld him, even when he was deepest sunk in helplessness, and he would go down under cover of darkness to look at the old, patient, unembittered face of his mother, and sometimes he would go to bed with a half-born resolution, since he was cast there, to stay there and share their fate, and not try to breathe an air that was thin for him and would stifle them. Then would it come over him, with an awful sense of desolation, how unspeakably absurd were the high-wrought dreams that every thought of Anne once brought him. Where was the place for her? For the delicately nurtured, exquisitely dressed, fastidious girl who, with all the favor she had shown him, yet seemed as distant from the rough background that lay close behind his life, as though her home were the clouds and his the earth forever. But it was his second self that spoke in this way—the self that was born of contact with civilization; for, whether it be the pride of independence or the complacence of isolation, the mountaineer, recognizing no social chasm, believes deep down in his heart that he is the peer of any and the inferior of none. Even with Stallard, this feeling was not dead, and, with him, in the end, little that was antagonism counted for more than the weight of a straw, when into one cup all his doubts, speculations, and purposes were strained at last—the cup of fatalism, from which he had drunk deep at birth, in his rearing, from the grim mountains that had cradled him—the draught that gave him his strength and drove him forward when, without it, he would have shrunk back and would have passed from the earth to count for little more on the stage of action than the daily shadow of Black Rock to and fro across the Cumberland. What is to be, will be. He was not to blame that his ways were not the ways of his people; his aspirations were not his own—whence they came, God only knew. He had not striven to gain Anne Bruce's favor. He had not asked to take another place than the place to which he was born. He had asked nothing of friend or foe, and he had nothing to ask now. Fate had put him where he was; fate might take him out: very well, he would go. And whether he went or stayed, he would do his duty just the same. Such was his final thought; and no man ever watched for the gleam that flashes from within as Boone Stallard hearkened to the inner voice that had but to whisper to be obeyed. The people wanted him to go back to the capital; very well, he would go back. That was what he told the Stallards at the courthouse one Saturday afternoon, and when he started for home, his brain swam with the thought of what must come. Responsibility had ceased for him—it was fate pointing the way beyond where he had dared to go. There was no turning back, then, when a little later came the crisis in his mountain life. Mace Keaton appeared one morning against the express terms of the truce—drunk and defiant. More, a little later he announced himself as a candidate to oppose Boone Stallard; more still, day by day the startling rumor that the Keatons meant to uphold his return and support his claim crystallized into certain fact. There was no doubt that Mace Keaton was acting from bitter personal hatred of Boone, and the Stallard leaders watched the latter closely and with fear. Always he had steered his course clear of the bloody run of feudal feeling. His acceptance of the nomination meant open enmity to the Keatons, open arrayal with them; it would make him the Stallard leader for the years to come. And they knew that he knew the penalty of his choice. Apparently he took no time to make up his mind. Straight and clear came his answer at once—he would run: the Stallards wanted him; Mace Keaton had violated the bond and so had his friends; the one had no right there—his friends no right to stand by him when he was plainly in the wrong.

It was a jubilee for the Stallards—this dictum. And all at once the burden of leadership, the responsibility of it and the terrible risk, were shifted in a day from shoulders that had long borne them to shoulders that had been well trained by other burdens to take on more—if more had to be borne. The truce not to take up arms held; and the Keatons felt honor bound to keep the more rigidly to it in other particulars, having so grossly violated it in one. So the conflict began peaceably enough. But the convention was to come, and nobody had a doubt as to what that would bring to pass. Boone Stallard was in the feud at last.

XII

CHRISTMAS passed and the time was nigh. The House was open; new matting had been laid; there were divans in the lobbies; the cloak-rooms and the library were fresh and clean and the flags were newly furled. In the Lower House a good-looking mulatto was tacking to the desks cards that bore the members' names. A portrait of Washington hung above the dingy gold eagle on the Speaker's chair. To his right Daniel Boone sat on a log in a sylvan bower, cocking his rifle — with a vista, cut by the artist, through thick woods to the placid Ohio. To the left was Lafayette, hat in hand, and strolling near a cliff that his preoccupation made perilous. Each picture was ticketed, perhaps to save unwary rustics the mortification that the memories of innocent questions would later bring. A few old members were writing in their seats. A pompous new one was walking around his desk, looking at his own name openly once, then furtively again and again.

Passing the Senate door, one saw the tall portrait of the great Commoner, his face smiling but imperious. Visitors were coming up and going down the oval stone stairway. Out on the steps was a "lady candidate" for librarian, with an imitation seal-skin thrown back and a bunch of carnations at her breast—smiling up into the flattered eyes of a very old statesman. Pushing a wheelbarrow towards the old iron gate was a trusty in stripes—a sullen fellow with a heavy jaw and a disfigured face. Over in the gray hotel of Kentucky marble, a crowd of tobacco-chewing politicians were wrangling about the Speakership for the coming term. The parlor was full of their wives and children. Outside, the day was clear, cloudless, brilliant, and warm, though along the road the moss was sprinkled with snow, and the hollows in the black hay-stacks out in the brown fields were plump and white. Out there the hazels, like the trees, were bending from the west—bent by the wind that blows ever from the sun. The far distance was hazy, dreamlike, reminiscent, and the mood of the horizon caught Anne when she turned with Katherine, on the hill, to look at the yellow western light, and held her while she walked back to the smoky town. Marshall was back; so was Stallard. No opponent dared to face Marshall in his own party, and the conflict in his county of rock-ribbed democracy was always, for the other side, a matter merely of form. So far there had never been any need for him to take a thought for his political morrow, and, as usual, he stayed quietly at home, and passed, as usual, into his honors without opposition.

It was Colton who had told her about Stallard. He had got the story from Jack Mockaby, a mountain member who had been at the convention in Roland. Stallard stormed through the little court-house like a mad lion, shaking his finger in Mace Keaton's face, defying him and his clan; and the magnificent audacity of the performance so dazed his adversaries that they finally led Keaton from the court-house and left the nomination to Stallard, at the cost of a lifetime of peace, at the cost some day of his life, maybe. He was openly the leader of the Stallards now. Pistols were drawn that day after the Keatons came out from the spell of Stallard's cyclonic oratory, and it was all but necessary for Boone to take up a gun, for the first time in his life, against his fellow-man. At the last moment, Stallard had even been in doubt about leaving home for the capital, questioning whether his duty were at one place or the other. Any day he might need to go back to a mortal conflict; and then, in the words of the mountain member which were familiar in Anne's memory, "there'd be Billy-hell to pay when he did." Marshall knew all this, and already it was plain that he and Stallard would be contestants for the Speakership. The old fight for disruption would surely come up again, and before Anne's eyes was nowhere the light of peace. It was a strange wrench from the placid run of her own life—to have her sympathies drawn into such a current of mediæval barbarism. There had been a great deal in the papers about the feud: about the people who took part in it; the method of warfare—ambushing from behind trees, lying in wait along the roadside, calling men to their own doors and shooting them down; worse still, cowards who had a little money paying assassins a petty sum to do their bloody work. Usually, it was said, one faction of the two rarely resorted to these means, and in this feud the Stallards had kept aloof from such hideous practices. That helped check Anne's growing horror, but it was incredible barbarism, and when she went back to the Mansion there appeared, as if to clinch the truth of what she had read, the only figure she had ever seen that might embody such evil. The warden would send over another trusty to take young Buck's place, her father said, and next morning she saw at the gate the sinister face of the convict with the sunken cheek, and Anne was transfixed. He, too, was a mountaineer. Stallard was one possibility of that life—here was another. She had the man told that there was nothing for him to do; and it was on her lips to ask her father then and there just what young Buck had done, but her delicate honor forbade—that, Stallard was going to tell her.

Why, she asked herself, passionately, did he not wrench loose wholly from such a life and from such people? Already he had answered the question—without cowardice and disloyalty he could not. It was not till then that she fully realized the mountaineer's strange predicament: his duty lay where he was; and if he could shake himself free, what then? The instincts that go with birth, the traits of character that grow with the training of childhood, the graces and culture that come with later associations, could never be his. Without them he would always be at a conscious disadvantage, and his pride would allow him no peace. For there was nothing in Stallard of that lurking hatred of the born gentleman, which she had noticed in other self-made men: the bitter jealousy of him, the contemptuous disparagement of his high claims and exactions. The mountaineer's bitterness was that he had not had the chance to be and to become all that was possible for a man. He was doing his best to make good what had been denied him; he would always do that. But meanwhile—with lips sealed for some reason—he was as helpless in the web of circumstance as a fly in a spider's toils; and it was his own strength that bound him.

Stallard had not come to see her; she did not know that he would come, even if he were not so busy—if the stress of affairs were not so great. Both the men she had seen but once. She was standing on the steps of the Mansion when Marshall appeared on the other side of the street. She expected him to lift his hat and pass on, but, to her surprise, he had come across and shaken hands with fine control, and had asked that he might have a long talk with her soon. The days of thought and settled purpose had wrought their story that summer in his face, which was brown, ruddy, and firm. Some change had taken place in him which made her wonder; and some change had come over Stallard. Him she had seen from the drawing-room window. He, too, was passing by in deep thought, and the sight of his face choked her—so lean and worn was it. It had a hunted and wary look—Colton had spoken to her of that—the look of a man ever at high tension, on constant guard against an enemy, on guard for his life.

To everybody, the change in both was quickly apparent. Marshall had come back with the purpose of being considerate, temperate, and just. Stallard's timidity was gone. He had taken on a new front, he was aggressive at the start, and Marshall, to his surprise and vexation, found himself where he had always held Stallard—on the defensive. On the morning of the first day in the caucus, to decide certain preliminary matters, Marshall's hot temper flared up, and there was a lightning cross-fire between the two men. It was as plain as noonday that a clash would come. Marshall had become a little unpopular; his haughtiness offended some and his wealth others; some were jealous of him. These, with the following upon which Stallard could count, were enough to make the contest of grave doubt to Marshall's friends, and the situation did not help Marshall, who brooked such rivalry with little tolerance and little grace.

It was an old tale for that day, and one not impossible now. At first, Stallard declined to arm himself, though Mockaby told him to his face that he was a fool to go unarmed. Neither meant to make an attack; both believed an attack possible; both used the plea of self-defence; and when, at the afternoon session, the lie all but passed, each man went armed the next day, and the close friends of each were in an unrest of expectancy. And on that day Anne's life began to be a melodrama which she would have ridiculed had it passed before her on the stage. At noon she heard that trouble was likely, and her father told her that ladies would not be allowed to enter the house that afternoon. So she stayed at home and, as women must, lay in a dark room with dry eyes and nothing to do but fear and think.

Meanwhile Marshall had spoken once, briefly and bitterly. Stallard replied briefly in kind, but with a cool moderation that inflamed Marshall more than bitterness could. As Marshall arose again, a messenger-boy laid a telegram on the mountaineer's desk. Colton saw him start, quickly break open the yellow envelope — and then saw every particle of color leave his face. There was but one answer for Stallard when Marshall sat down, and had the listeners been forced to sit still, while a bolt of lightning played under the ceiling, the face of every man could hardly have been more intense, nor would Marshall's, had he known that it was he whom the bolt would strike. There was but one answer to Stallard, too, and Marshall's white silence was an omen that the answer was sure to come. He went out before the session was quite over, and Mockaby, preceding Stallard a step, saw him waiting near one of the gray pillars at the far end of the portico, and gave the mountaineer a nod of warning. Stallard purposely walked towards the other end, and as he stepped down on the brick flagging, Marshall stepped down, too, facing him. Men near each of them scurried quickly out of line. The members coming out stopped still about the pillars, and Marshall's voice cut clearly through the sudden quiet.

"Stallard," he called, reaching for his pistol, "we'd as well settle this thing now."

Stallard saw the movement and, mountaineerlike, thought Marshall meant to get the advantage. Like lightning his own weapon flashed, and the two reports

"HE TOSSED HIS WEAPON ASIDE"

struck Mockaby's ear as one. It was hasty work, and both missed. Marshall's revolver spoke again, as he fired, advancing. Stallard hitched one shoulder slightly and, to Mockaby's terror, looked down at his pistol, his face unmoved. Hearing no other shot, he looked up again quickly, and stood motionless and bewildered, staring at Marshall. Mockaby, too, was staring helplessly; for Marshall, seeing the trouble with the mountaineer's pistol, was quietly waiting for him to get ready again.

Stallard reddened and looked shamed; then, with a turn of his wrist, he tossed his weapon aside. It rang on the flagging at Mockaby's feet, and Mockaby stooped mechanically to pick it up. When he rose upright, he saw Stallard striding towards Marshall with his hand outstretched. Promptly Marshall stepped forward to meet him, shifting his pistol as he came, and, midway, the two men caught hands. It was too much for the on-lookers: the strain of mortal expectancy; the gallant magnanimity of the one, the perfect courage of the other. Mockaby was struck dumb, but a hum of enthusiasm rose behind him. One old Confederate, who had stood at rigid attention against a pillar, was wiping his eyes, and his mouth was twitching; and, as Stallard walked towards the gate, a policeman held it open for him, and touched his corded slouch hat as the mountaineer passed through.

An hour later, he was at the post-office eagerly breaking the seal of a letter from home. He read it once, and, leaning against the railing, read it again, with his face quite expressionless. Then he took his hat off and walked bareheaded up the street. The warning clang of a coming train brought him sharply up as he started across the track, and, reaching for his watch, he found his hat still in his hand. With a shake of his shoulders, he hurried to the Governor's office.

In a little while he came out again with a set face and started for his room. At the steps of the Mansion he looked at his watch for the third time on his way that far, and with the hesitation of a moment rang the bell. He told the negro girl who opened the door to say to her mistress that he was going away, and had only a minute in which to say good-bye. The girl shrank from him, and Anne, who happened to be starting down-stairs, could not tell what he said, and hardly knew his voice. Coming in from the strong light so suddenly, he did not see her; so, with a nod to the servant, she let him pass into the drawing-room without calling to him, and stopped an instant at the foot of the stairs, her clasp tightening on the banisters. She had just heard of the all but mortal meeting of the two men—her eyes were still wet with tears of relief. Marshall had just sent her word that he was coming to the Mansion in an hour, and she was wondering why. Why was Stallard here?

The mountaineer had not sat down when she passed in. He was at the window, and he heard her coming and turned quickly. He did not offer to shake hands—he made no greeting, but stood silent, his body swaying slightly, as it did when he was greatly moved, and he looked as he looked the first time she saw him in the State House, and Anne felt the warning flutter of some new terror and steeled herself.

"I'm going home to-night," he said. "I may not come back very soon . . . I may not come back at all. And I've come to tell you good-bye. It's come down in the mountains. They've killed two of my cousins. They've sent me word"—the curious little zigzag streaks of red began to run up and down his cheeks when he stopped to gain self-control—"that they will sell my mother's cattle, and—and hire out my sister. Your father says he can't help me. So it all depends on me, and I'm going to-night—in an hour. I don't know that I'll get back ... the chances are that I sha'n't ... so there's no need yet to tell you the one thing that I've kept from you ... that I've kept from everybody ... here. I shall tell it, if I come back; and then, if you can forgive that, I may have something to ask you. I can't speak the words now, and how I shall ever dare to say them, I don't know. I am crazy now, I think ... but you know, you *must* know. I am helpless before you—like a child. You have been very good to me, and I have told you all but one thing. I've kept that back ... from everybody ... but I shall tell it ... to you. I'm going now. I have given my word to the people there, and I'm going to keep it. You are the one person on earth to me ... besides my mother and sister ... the rest of the world is nothing ... and if you can forgive one thing more, as you have forgiven so much,

I . . . I shall make myself worthy. How I shall work for that. Good-bye . . . if I don't come back . . . you will know why . . . good-bye."

Already he was starting for the door, while the girl stood silent, cold, white. To save her soul she could not utter a word, and, like a statue, she watched him leave with a broken "God bless you" that gave her a throb of pain to hear. She heard the door close, his heavy tread across the porch, and she followed, opening the door and looking down the street where he had disappeared. She saw a figure coming towards her, but not until it had halted at the bottom of the steps was she aware that it was Marshall, smiling up at her. It was surprising that he should appear just at that moment; she had forgotten that he was to come, though she still held his note in her hand. She saw a keen, curious look flit through his eyes, and she felt the rush of tears on her face. Then her father spoke from the corner of the steps below — she had not seen him at all.

"You will win to-morrow," he said to Marshall. "Your rival has fled. There's trouble in Roland, and Stallard came to me for soldiers. Of course I couldn't help him—nor could I help approving his plan to take the matter in hand himself. I don't blame him. It looks pretty serious—Why, Anne!"

Then all at once Marshall seemed to understand; for an instant Anne helplessly met his sharp, straight gaze, and before she could speak, he was lifting his hat and turning away. She started indoors then, swerving slightly, and her father caught her arm, thinking that she had tripped on something and was about to fall.

Stallard did not appear in the House next morning. Just before the vote for Speaker was cast the chairman read to the astonished members the withdrawal from the race, for reasons to be hereafter explained, of the member from Roland. There was not a vote against Marshall, and next day the papers made public the reason of Stallard's absence. Mace Keaton had control of Roland with his faction, and was in open defiance. Stallard had sent in to the Governor his resignation from the House, and had then gone down to make good his word that his people could take care of themselves. A desperate fight was imminent any hour.

XIII

To meet death a rat goes to his hole, a lion to his lair; the same instinct, perhaps, in the shadow of a lesser crisis even, sends a man home. Marshall took the train with Anne's face still haunting him like the face of the dead. Chance had rent the veil, and he had turned away, as he would have turned had chance as suddenly bared the girl's breast as it had seemed to bare her soul. The stupefying calm that held him broke slowly as the train rushed through the winter fields; and slowly his hold on himself began to loosen. By the time he was climbing into his buggy he was asking himself fiercely what the use of it all was; and, a moment later, he pulled his mare to her haunches before his club door, in answer to an old voice within him that had been still for a long while. He had always stopped there in the old days, and it was the habit of resisting the impulse since those days, perhaps, that made him suddenly lash his horse on now. The mare sprang ahead with a frightened snort, and Marshall, with a half-curse on himself for his thoughtless cruelty, called kindly to her several times to make recompense. Then he settled back into his big coat, and, a little later, he was on the white turnpike again speeding home, with his chin on his breast and the same fight in his soul that was there on that other drive, when Stallard first came into his life and into Anne's. Only the yellow evening light was almost gone now. There was not a bird-note from the darkening brown fields. The sun was a sullen blotch of fire when he reached his gate, and the woods behind the house were black and still. But his mother was waiting for him, and he was very tender with her that night. She knew something was wrong—she always knew; but she waited for him to tell, as she always did; and there were things that he had never told and could never tell, which she never knew nor guessed; and he was grateful, whatever the shame her faith and his weakness brought to him. The pantry door was open when he went to his room, but there was no glisten of glassware from within. That temptation had been removed long ago, and it was well for him that night that it was. His room was cold; the white moon through the window looked cold, and the dead fields and the gaunt moonlit woods. The whole world was cold, and every riotous drop in the veins of his reckless forefathers was running wild in his, when he went sleepless to bed and to an all-night struggle that sent him groping back through his past for the things that were the stay of his unthinking childhood. For the first time in years, he was ready to go with his mother to church next morning when the carriage drove before the door. It was a sign to her of some unusual distress of mind, and a grateful surprise that she was too wise to show. Instinctively she took him to the old country church where she used to take him when he was a boy; and, going and coming, the little school-house where he and Anne had been playmates gave him a sharp pang; but the old church that had brought its sturdy walls and sturdy faith down from the pioneers, the saddle-horses hitched to the plank fence, the long stiles, with the country girls dismounting in their long black skirts, the atmosphere of reverence, the droning old hymns—all helped little by little to draw him back to the faith from which he had started adrift; to stir memories that were good for him, and to make easier what was to come. From church, several neighbors went home with them to dinner, after a custom of the neighborhood; and it was after they were gone that a negro boy brought the morning paper to Marshall's room. He opened it, and read one paragraph on the first page twice—then he threw the paper on the table and rose. It was a terse telegram from Stallard to the Governor. The fight was over, and Stallard was safe and successful. And he was coming back. Marshall's acceptance of the fact and its probable significance was quick, proud, and fiery. Only he picked up his hat and got quickly out into the open air. His mother was in the front yard, and he did not want to see her quite yet; so he went into the parlor, where a fire was still burning, and sat down by the window — forestalling the days that were at hand. He was before Anne now, paying her his tribute to Stallard; and from the depths of his unworthy satire rose the bitter fact that what he was saying to himself, and mentally to Anne, was literal truth—the mountaineer *was* worthy. And with this realization, he suddenly lost the power to feel the thousand subtleties that he had always believed would prevent Anne from joining her life to Stallard's, no matter what her admiration for him, her respect, her pity, or even her love.

Then, for the first time in his life, jealousy started throbbing through him, and he knew the hell of two passions fighting his soul at once. It stretched him out on the sofa where he sat, and he lay there a long time, dully watching the evening sunlight as it rose slowly to the face of his boyish uncle on the wall, whose life and death was a tragedy that seemed meant for him to play again. He looked with a deeper sympathy now behind the smiling lips and the reckless smiling eyes, and with a throb of pity for him which was half for himself, he hurried out into the woods and the dusk.

THE KENTUCKIANS

It was startling to realize that nothing, not even religion nor his mother, had governed his life as had his love of Anne. Without her, it seemed that he must lose anchor and go adrift. And once, in the night, sick with fever and mad for a little relief, he sprang from his bed to take his buggy and go back to town and lose himself in the old way. This time it was the swift vision of his mother's face that stopped him in the middle of the floor—his duty was to her now—and forced him in an agony of helplessness to his knees in the first prayer that had been wrung from him in years. That was his crucial hour, and he faced the morning, grateful; but he stayed at home that day through distrust of himself—and to keep away from the capital.

Life had almost begun anew for him a year ago; he believed now that, without Anne, it must begin quite new. It was like walking back into childhood when he started out after breakfast on foot, and every memory was a healing comfort. When he passed the spring-house, the geese raised their wings with a reedy cackling and, with the ducks, went swinging down the riffles, as though they yet expected him to throw pebbles at them. At the stone fence, beyond, he stopped to look at the water bubbling over the water-gap, through which he used to drop his hook for perch and catfish. Then he followed the winding branch by a pig-path, through the thickly matted long grass, that was criss-crossed by tiny beaten roads that used to lead many a musk-rat to death in his traps. A hawk was sweeping the field with his wings, hovering close to the grass in his hunt for a breakfast of mice. The old impulse came to run back to the house for his gun, and the gray bird swerved like a glancing arrow to safety on a dead tree far out in the meadow. Up in the sun, the hill-side was covered with sheep.

THE KENTUCKIANS

A ewe with one white lamb was lapping water at the grassy edge of the creek. Just to one side of the path lay another—its twin, no doubt—dead and mutilated, and across the creek hung its murderer, a robber crow, dangling by his wings from a low limb, with his penitent beak between his feet.

He was not the only thing on earth that had to suffer. Life was a chain of suffering, with nature at one end and nature at the other; a pyramid of cruelty with man at the apex exacting the tribute of sacrifice from below, paying it right and left to the strong, and above to the unseen. He must take his share. There were other motives to action in life than love, than duty to his mother—the duty to those of whom he had not thought much, and of whom suffering was teaching him to think now: others than himself—his duty to the world around, above and below. He might have drawn tears from an audience on that theme once with his tongue and his brain: it was sinking to his heart now.

Anne was right; he had made a wretched use of himself. He had been weak and reckless, and wasteful of the time, energy, and the talents, whatever they were, that God had given him. He had made of his love a moping luxury instead of a motive to deeds that were worth doing; he was selfish and degenerate. He loved his State, he thought, and he was intensely proud of it and of his people. Yet there was Stallard fighting like a savage on its border— that was a stain; and there was he provoking the same man to a deadly conflict at the very seat of order and law. Where was the difference, except that the mountaineer, as he claimed, had the better right to fight in the one place and, as Marshall admitted, the better excuse in the other. It was hypocrisy for him to blame Stallard and to justify himself. Courage was a passionate ideal in him, as it is in his people. Human life was worth less, he believed, and was proud that his State believed, and would not have it otherwise, than certain old-fashioned ideals that were still all-powerful; but was it not possible to lift life and yet not lower those ideals at all? That was something he might have helped to do. Once, a political career was an honored one. He could help bring the honor of it back. There were consolations, too—the thrill of power as a speaker, the exhilaration of conflict, the pride in a good cause—ah! there was much left in the world, even after love was gone out.

All these years it had taken him to realize simple facts about which he had thundered with such confidence in college; and now, far out in the woods, he lay on a stone wall in the warm sun, taking in the comfort of his discovery, until the mellow tone of the dinner-bell rang noon across the fields. From everywhere came answering shouts from the darkies at work; and when he climbed the yard fence going home he could hear the jingling traces of the plough-horses crowding into the barnyard, and the laughing banter of the darkies about the whitewashed cabins. It was all very busy and peaceful and comforting, and it was his to have day after day, when he pleased.

And so, that afternoon, it seemed a bigger and a kindlier world when he started out again through the winter blue-grass, past the white tobacco-barn, past the spring in the woods, gushing from under a rock over rich, bent grass, May-green; on over brown turf and under gray woods to the "field" where the breakers were at work. How he would fool the birds that croaked evil of him! All over the hillside the hemp lay in shining swaths. Two darkies were picking it up with wooden hooks; another was working at a brake, which, at that distance, looked absurdly like a big doll-baby with tow-linen skirts blowing in the wind. The rest were idling about a fire of hurds. The overseer stood near with his hand outstretched, as though he were arguing. He was having trouble of some kind, for but one other negro was at work, an old fellow with gray whiskers, thick lips, and a striped over-suit of cotton. Nobody could hear Marshall's tread on the thick turf.

"Hemp gone down, boys," the overseer was saying. "Can't pay you more—sorry. If you don't like the price, you needn't work. Nobody's feelin's hurt. Brakes won't go beggin'."

The old darky picked on. The brawny breaker swooped up a fresh armful with his left hand, and, with his right, brought the heavy upper swords crackling down on the stiff stalks until his figure was lost in a gray cloud of hurds.

"Dat's right," said one of the idlers. "I ain't gwine to wuck."

"All right," said the overseer. "Hit the pike. Nobody's feelin's hurt. Brakes won't go beggin'. Could 'a' got hands in town yesterday, but wanted to give you boys a chance. Hit the pike."

The man at the brake seemed not to hear. His hemp had got bright and flexible, and it sank like folds of iron-gray hair down through the lower swords, which were smooth, shining, and curved like the throat of a harp. The idlers had all started from the fire, but only one reached the fence at the pike, and he turned on the top rail and looked back. Slowly, one after another, the men were going to work. It was Marshall's own orders that the shrewd overseer had given the simple negroes. There was another thing that he might have done than cut their wages down—he could have taken less profit for himself—and he did that now.

"Give them the old price," he called, in

a low voice, but they heard, and a row of white teeth shone in every black face. It was to him like light to darkness—that grateful flash. It helped the deeps to open as he turned away. Love was not everything. All day that fact had beat in on him persistently, and it was strange that never once came with it the suspicion that Anne too might know that, with a man, love should not be everything; that she might be generous enough to accept the fact; unselfish enough to exact it of him; that his love for her was a weakness that kept her from perfect respect for him as long as it kept him from paying the debt that he owed to his State, his name, and to himself; and that, being a goal in itself, her love might lose value when he had gained it. Stallard was coming back. Until Anne should open her lips, it was no more his business than if he had never known her. Again and again the thought had forced itself on him, with some bitterness, that she had not been altogether just and frank. Now he straightway gave her absolution. Women did not understand friendship as men did; besides, both were not friends — he was a lover. She may not have wanted to pain him. The flash may have come to her as to him from a clear sky. But it had come, and his way was straight, and it led him into a calm that was like the quiet sunset that he faced, turning homeward.

Away off in the east, across the gently concave sky, some little blue clouds had begun to turn golden. The air had grown cold and the shadows long. The crows were coming home to roost; there was a line of black specks across the low even band of yellow that lay across the west like a stubble wheat-field at noon. Against this the trees, with trunks invisible, were set bright, sharp, and clear; and when he reached the brow of a low hill he saw, black and distinct against the after-glow, the last of the many pictures that were etched on his brain that day to stay—the dim sloping barn, the black cedars with one light shining through them, and, above, the roof that sheltered his mother, his father's memory, and a name of which, henceforth, please God, he should make himself worthy.

At once he put his purpose to a bitter test, when he reached the darkened house, by going up-stairs and straight to his book of memories. And there, in the dusk, he tore out the leaves one by one and heaped them in the grate. Then he set them afire and left the room that he might not see them burn.

The blaze lit up the room and showed the picture of Anne on the mantel—in white muslin, with a blue ribbon about her throat and a Leghorn hat in her lap. It showed, too, the paper on the table, where Marshall had thrown it the day before, and by the light one could have read Stallard's message to the Governor — it was as laconic as Cæsar's:

"I told you I should retake my fireside. It's done."

XIV

COLTON himself had gone to the scene of the conflict, and, on the second day, the people in the capital read the story of the fight: and nothing was lost to it, nor to Stallard, in the telling. Colton had got the mountaineer's terse message to the Governor, and the ring of it and the passion for analogy spun the story around a circuit that made Stallard notorious. The mountaineer had led his law-and-order party into the town, as a sheriff's posse, at daybreak. At that hour the sheriff disappeared and Stallard alone was in command. His coolness, witnesses said, was extraordinary. One man had seen him stop shooting in the heat of the fight, deliberately touch the muzzle of his Winchester to the ground, and, while two Keatons were cross-firing at him, deliberately resume again. He was nervous, he explained afterwards, having been without sleep and on an intense strain for forty-eight hours, and he had been told that, in a fight, it would calm a man simply to touch his gun to the earth. Evidently it did calm him, for at his first shot thereafter a Keaton dropped to the ground with a broken shoulder. Mace Keaton and three others would give no further trouble, Colton concluded; and, indeed, the feud in that county was done. The intimidated were plucking up heart, and the good men of the county were taking Stallard's part. Several ringleaders had been arrested, and would be sent to the blue-grass for trial. Boone Stallard had made his word good.

That afternoon Marshall asked that his old bill for disruption be voted down, gave Stallard a eulogy, and went home, half ill.

THE KENTUCKIANS

The House entered a unanimous protest against the mountaineer's resignation of his seat, though Colton had written that Stallard would return to the capital for only a few days, and would go back, then, where he was needed—home.

A week later, Marshall and the mountaineer reached the capital on the same day. As the purpose of both was the same, it was not unnatural that, when Marshall came to see Anne in the afternoon, she should have just received a note from Stallard, asking if he could come that night. She was in the haze of great mental distress when Marshall's name was brought to her; she was stifling for the open air, and the day was a sunny promise of spring—a day that may stand sharply out in any season as a forecast of the next to come. So Anne came down dressed for a walk, and it was a trick of the fate whose hand seemed ever at Stallard's throat that led the three together on the hill.

As they passed through the old bridge they met several people driving—so warm was the air—and when they turned off from the river, Anne directed Marshall's attention up the hill and smiled.

"I'm not as freakish as you might think," she said.

Colton and Katherine were far above them, walking slowly, and when they reached the curve of the road, Colton was waving at them from the other end of the segment and close to the crest of the hill. Twice he pointed significantly towards the road below him, and, in a moment, Anne saw why. Stallard's tall figure was moving slowly up the pike, with his hands clasped behind him, and his head bent far over. The gate at the oak-tree was opposite, and Anne turned towards it from the road. Marshall, seeing Stallard just then, knew why, and turned, too, without a word. Had a thunder-cloud swept suddenly over the sun, the day could not have been more swiftly darkened for both; for Anne's silent recoil was to Marshall another surprised confession, however vague, and had Anne but glanced at him she would have known that with him, too, a decisive moment was at hand. She could not help looking back, even after she had passed through the gate and was following Marshall up the path. The mountaineer had turned, and was walking down the road, his figure unchanged. While she looked, he slowly turned again, as though he were pacing to and fro, waiting for some one. He looked weak and he looked wretched, and the girl's breath came hard. The mountaineer had come back to tell her what she already knew, that Buck, the young trusty who had worked in her garden, was the brother of whom he had spoken, and to ask her—what? And what should she say? It was plain now—his course from the beginning: his struggle with his duty to his people, his temptation to hide from the world the one thing that he had left untold to her. If she forgave that—and she had—he meant to ask her—she well knew what—and what should she say? What could she say? For days she had not been able to think of anything else—she could think of nothing else now. The horror of it all had swept freshly over her after the relief of Stallard's safety came—horror at what he had done, though she knew she would have despised him had he even hesitated doing it; horror at the life with which he was so mercilessly linked, of which she knew so little, and from which she was beginning to shrink as she shrank from the terrible convict who typified to her all the evil she had heard, and was the one distinct figure in the awful darkness of which she dreamed. And yet, one by one, the barriers that would have made Stallard's question absurd a year ago had slowly fallen until now it troubled her as nothing else of the kind ever had. Never had love in another man thrilled her as it thrilled her in Stallard—that much was sure. She had for him perfect respect, high admiration, deep pity — what else more she did not know.

It was odd that Marshall should stop at the same tree where she and Stallard had stopped nearly a year before; that she should sit quite mechanically on the same root where she had sat before; odd that he should lie where Stallard had lain. The contrast was marked now between the clean, graceful figure stretched easily on the sun-warmed, yellow grass and the loose, powerful bulk of the mountaineer. She remembered Stallard's unshorn head, looking now at Marshall's carefully kept brown hair. The sunlight showed its slight tendency to crinkle; she had always hated that, but no more, she knew, than did he. It was odd that so slight a thing should so worry her now. The faces of both were smooth, and, to Anne's searching insight, the life of both was written plain, except for one dark spot from which, in each, she shrank. It had kept her from fully trusting one; it had held her sometimes in an unaccountable dread of the other. Marshall was not gaining ground as he lay there with his hat tilted over his eyes and a blade of withered grass between his teeth—easy, indolent, an image to her of wasting power—for Anne was thinking of Stallard down in the road, and it was well for him that he began to speak. No woman could listen with indifference to a voice that was so rich and low.; that told all the good in him and none of the evil.

"Anne," he said, and the girl raised her head quickly. She could hardly remember when he had called her by her first name, and the tone of his voice was new. "Anne," he repeated, with a firm note of possession, as it seemed to her, that made her pulse with sudden resentment, "I am done now."

His tone was almost harsh, and he was not looking at her, but at a vivid patch of young wheat that glanced like an emerald on the brown top of a distant sunlit hill. And Anne, looking hard at him, saw again the change that the summer had brought. The fieriness was gone from him, and the old impetuous way of breaking into a torrent of words, and as suddenly breaking off in a useless effort to frame thought and feeling. He looked as calm as a young monk she had once seen at Gethsemane—as calm as though his peace, too, was made for earth as well as heaven.

"Let me see. It must have been ten years ago. It was coming home through the woods from the old school-house. I had a red welt on my forehead. I told you I had got it playing town-ball—that was not true. I got it fighting about you. It was Indian-summer, I recollect that, and sunset—you remember, don't you?"

"Yes," she said, wonderingly and almost gently; but she was thinking, too, of Stallard going up and down the road —he looked lonely.

"I asked you to be my sweetheart, and I was just sixteen." Marshall might have been repeating words that had been carefully prepared, so finished were his sentences, so dramatic the quality of them. "and you said 'yes'; yes, you said 'yes'; and that was ten years ago, and I have never loved another woman since. I have made no pretence of loving another; or of not loving one. When I came home from college, something had happened, and you began to say 'no'; but I kept on loving you just the same—and you kept on saying 'no.' I am doing the one thing now, and you are still doing the other. Ten years! That gives me some rights, little as I may otherwise deserve them, doesn't it, Anne?" The voice was doing good work now.

"Yes, Rannie," she said, and she had

never called him by that name since he went away to school; but if he noticed it, he gave no sign. The green on the hilltop still held his eyes, and for a moment he said nothing. The sunlight was very rich for midwinter, as rich as though it had been sifted through gold-dust somewhere. It seemed palpable enough to grasp with the hand across the running water that was making it pulse in quivering circles along bush and tree. It foretold an early spring, and made Anne think of the shy green of young leaves and the gold of the same sunlight a year ago, and then of Stallard, through the soft gray cloud of winter trees, walking up and down the road, waiting.

"I'm going to take them now. People inherit tendencies to go down."

Anne turned to him again: he was speaking of himself, and he had never done that before but once.

"Everybody knows and remembers that.

People may, at the same time, inherit the aspiration for better things and the strength to rise to them. Everybody seems to forget that, sometimes—even you. And yet you were right, and I haven't a word of blame."

Nor had he, she recalled quickly, that night after the dance, when, losing patience, she had broken out with her defence of Stallard. She remembered now the start her outburst gave him, the quick flush of his face, his quick restraint, and the steady quiet with which he had unflinchingly taken to heart the bitter truth she gave him, and his courtesy to the end. She was too much aroused that night to care what pain she caused him, but the memory of it hurt her now.

"You have been hard, but you have not been unjust. I have been fighting a long time, and you might have given me a little more credit for the fight. I think you would have given me more, if you had cared more. Because you seemed not to care, I did not ask it. It was a weakness to want it . . . I don't need it now . . . whatever happens, I shall keep my own path just the same . . ."

Anne hardly took in what he was saying, his voice was so dispassionate. Marshall had always been generous, winning, faithful—that was what she was thinking. Why had she never loved *him*? It was as strange as that she should not know what it was she felt for Stallard.

"For I'm done now," repeated Marshall, inexorably. "I'm going to take my rights. I'm going to leave you altogether."

She heard now, and she turned, half dazed. Marshall was steeling himself against his own tenderness and going calmly on:

"When you want me, if you ever do, you must send for me. It is all, or nothing, I must have. And you must give it unasked now, if you should ever have it to give. Yes," he went on, as though to answer her unuttered cry of surprise and indignation . . . "I know your pride —your foolish, steely pride—but I'm done now."

Anne's eyes were wide with bewilderment. Was he gone crazy?

"I have loved you for ten years. I don't wonder at your distrust of me, but it's different now. Perhaps you don't yet trust me? In that event, I don't care how long a test you put upon me. Only, if by some miracle you should want me to come back, you will have no right to say, 'Maybe he has ceased to care for me now.' You will have no right to say that, even to yourself — to think it. I promise, if that ever happens, to come and tell you myself. I promise that. I have done all I can—all I should. The rest is with you now, wholly."

Marshall was rising. He had not looked

at her since he began to talk — he had hardly dared for fear his purpose should fail him — and Anne rose too, as though he had bidden her.

"If you marry anybody else, I'll wait for him to die. You can't escape me in the end." He was smiling faintly, but his tone was almost rough, and Anne was ready both to laugh and to cry. "And I'll never come till you send for me. We'd better go now," he said, coolly, and he started down, Anne following, quite helpless, without a word, and with a growing sense of desertion that oppressed her and made her unconsciously look for Stallard when they emerged from the undergrowth. She was quite sure she would see him, and there he was, walking rapidly past the gate, but he did not seem to see them, so intent was he on something down the road. Her dress caught on a bush, as Marshall pulled back the gate, and, when he stooped to disentangle it, she heard the mountaineer's voice around a clump of bushes below them. Marshall rose quickly, and, the next moment, both heard what he was saying.

"No," he said, sternly. "I'll give you the money, but you must go back. I got you out, and I gave my word you wouldn't run away. You've *got* to go back."

A rough voice, strangely like his own to the girl's ears, answered something unintelligible.

"Then I'll take you back myself."

A low oath of rage and the shuffling of feet came through the bushes, and Marshall caught Anne's arm.

"You stay here," he said, firmly, and he hurried through the gate and around the bushes. Stallard was blocking the road against a rough-looking fellow, who started to run when he saw Marshall. Stallard caught him by the arm, and with the other hand the fellow struck the mountaineer a fearful blow in the face.

"... I KNOW WHAT YOU THOUGHT."

"God, man!" shouted Marshall, indignantly; for, to his amazement, Stallard did not give back the blow but caught his assailant by the other wrist.

"Come here and help," he said. "This is an escaped convict."

Marshall ran forward, and the convict gave up and dropped stubbornly to the road, coughing hard, crying from rage, and cursing Stallard by his first name.

"You're a fine brother, hain't ye?" he repeated, with savage malice, starting another string of curses and stopping short, with his eyes fixed on something behind Stallard. The mountaineer wheeled. Anne was standing there, her face quite bloodless, and her eyes wide and full upon his.

"You heard what he said?"

It was the mountaineer's voice that broke at last through the awful silence, and in this test, even, it was steady.

"I know what you thought. This—this is my brother."

Anne's eyes turned slowly to the convict, who lay at Stallard's feet with his sunken cheek towards her; and slowly the truth forced its terrible way to her brain and then back again to Stallard in one look of unspeakable horror, unspeakable pity.

"This was what I had to tell you," he said, quietly; but his face had whitened quickly, all but the red welt where the convict had struck. "I have nothing to ask—now." Not in voice or bearing was there the slightest reproach for her.

"Get up, Bud," he said, kindly. Anne turned for an instant to Marshall, when the convict rose, but it was a second rending of the veil for him, and he had moved away that he might not hear. Before the two could take a step, she was at the mountaineer's side.

"I . . . I'm—going with you!"

Marshall heard that and, but for his agitated face, Stallard's calm must have broken. For he understood, even then, what was beyond Marshall to know, and at that moment, perhaps, beyond Anne. She had struck into his heart when he was most helpless, and, to atone, she would walk with him through the streets of the town, back to the very walls of the prison, on through life even, if he asked. All this Stallard saw—and more—and he shook his head.

"God bless you!" he said. . . . "Come on, Bud!"

The two brothers started down the road towards town — and towards the shifting black column of smoke that rose over the gray prison beyond.

A year later one of them, faithful to the end as the other's keeper, came to the capital to deliver his charge back to the Keeper of the things that die.

"If that had happened before—" said Katherine, questioningly; but Anne shook her head.

"Not that—not that," she said, sadly. "I don't know . . . I . . . " And there she stopped still.

A flood of development was at high tide in the mountains before another year was gone, and it seemed as though the prophecy of Stallard's first speech at the capital was coming true. His name was slowly radiating from the great capital then; and a year later still, Marshall rose as a senator of the State, and in a fervid piece of oratory, in which he was now without a rival, spoke for Boone Stallard for the Senate of the nation. Stallard was defeated; but when Katherine Colton, who was a guest at the Bruce homestead, told Anne of the quixotic fight that Marshall, to his own hurt, had made for the mountaineer, Anne let her head sink back out of the light into a shadow. Then

Katherine, who knew how matters stood between the two, spoke sharply and with the authority that had lately come to her. As a result, a night or two afterwards, a buggy creaked softly over the turf from the pike gate and a dark active figure climbed the stiles. Katherine rose for flight.

"Please . . ." said Anne, ". . . not yet."

From an up-stairs window, Katherine saw the moon rising on the two at the gate, and on the gracious sweep of field, meadow, and woodland that had always been and would always be, perhaps, his home and hers. Lying all along the east, and hardly touched as yet by the coming light, was a bank of dark clouds, as mountainlike and full of mystery as though they were faithful shadows of the great Range behind and beyond — and Katherine's eyes filled. When she went to bed she could hear the voices of the two now and then on the porch below, until she fell asleep. She felt a pair of arms around her next, and a pair of lips at her ear.

"Katherine!"

"Yes?" she said, sleepily.

Anne kissed her.

THE END

Printed in the United States
147813LV00008B/108/A